Steve and Pat Brock were plunged into an unspeakable nightmare July 27, 1986, with one shattering phone call that brought the mind-numbing, heartbreaking news: "There's been an accident . . . your son David is dead!"

The shock . . . the unbearable grief . . . the denial . . . the rage . . . the thoughts of suicide . . . and finally the road to inner healing and peace are charted in this true story, *Strength for Today, Bright Hope for Tomorrow.*

I recommend this book to all who are in search of healing from the deep wounds of unexplained and unspeakable tragedy.

—Pastor John Hagee, Cornerstone Church

In my office I frequently have opportunity to see firsthand the devastation of sudden and tragic loss in the death of an immediate family member. This is aggravated when a child is lost. It is natural for children to bury parents; it is not natural for parents to bury children. Steve and Pat Brock have provided a wonderful resource for parents in situations similar to theirs. I am sure that the sharing of their experience will help bring healing to many.

—Dr. Richard Dobbins, Emerge Ministries, Inc.

# STRENGTH
## FOR
# TODAY
## &
# BRIGHT HOPE
## FOR
# TOMORROW

### STEVE BROCK

THOMAS NELSON PUBLISHERS
Nashville • Atlanta • London • Vancouver

Published in Nashville, Tennessee, by Thomas Nelson, Inc., Publishers, and distributed in Canada by Word Communications, Ltd., Richmond, British Columbia, and in the United Kingdom by Word (UK), Ltd., Milton Keynes, England.

Unless otherwise noted Scripture quotations are from the NEW KING JAMES VERSION of the Bible. Copyright © 1979, 1980, 1982, 1990, 1994, Thomas Nelson, Inc., Publishers.

Scripture quotations noted NIV are from the HOLY BIBLE, NEW INTERNATIONAL VERSION ®. Copyright © 1973, 1978, 1984 by International Bible Society. Used by permission of Zondervan Publishing House. All rights reserved.

Scripture quotations noted NASB are from THE NEW AMERICAN STANDARD BIBLE ®, © Copyright The Lockman Foundation 1960, 1962, 1963, 1968, 1971, 1972, 1973, 1975, 1977. Used by permission.

The "NIV" and "New International Version" trademarks are registered in the United States Patent and Trademark Office by International Bible Society. Use of either trademark requires the permission of International Bible Society.

Scripture quotations noted KJV are from The Holy Bible, KING JAMES VERSION.

Scripture quotations noted TLB are from THE LIVING BIBLE (Wheaton, Illinois: Tyndale House Publishers, 1971) and are used by permission.

Scripture quotations noted J. B. PHILLIPS are from J.B. PHILLIPS: THE NEW TESTAMENT IN MODERN ENGLISH, Revised Edition. Copyright © J.B. Phillips 1958, 1960, 1972. Used by permission of Macmillan Publishing Co., Inc.

Scripture quotations noted CEV are from the CONTEMPORARY ENGLISH VERSION of the Bible © 1991, 1995 by the American Bible Society. Used by permission.

**Library of Congress Cataloging-in-Publication Data**
Brock, Steve.
    Strength for today, bright hope for tomorrow / Steve Brock.
        p.    cm.
    Includes bibliographical references.
    ISBN 0-7852-7557-6 (pbk.)
    1. Consolation. 2. Children—Death—Religious aspects—Christianity.
3. Bereavement—Religious aspects—Christianity. 4. Brock, Steve. I. Title.
BV4907.B76 1997
248.8'66—dc21                                       97-2907
                                                  CIP

Printed in the United States of America
1 2 3 4 5 6 7 BVG 01 00 99 98 97

## Dedication

Dedicated to my wife Pat,
whom I love so much and could not live without;

My son Tony, of whom I am so proud;

And to my son David,
whom I look forward to seeing just inside the pearly gates.

## Acknowledgments

A special thank-you to Pastor Benny Hinn, for without his inspiration and encouragement this book would never have come about; Jan Crouch who was there for me in my darkest hour; and Sheryl Palmquist for her direction and editorial assistance in developing this manuscript.

# CONTENTS

Losing a child is by far one of the greatest tragedies an individual can encounter in life. According to national statistics this is viewed by many as the greatest crisis a parent can face.

What happens when a father is notified that his teenage son has been killed? How can a man deal with such loss?

*Strength for Today, Bright Hope for Tomorrow* presents the real-life story of Steve Brock, a man who has walked this lonely road of grief and pain. His journey as a grieving father began on July 27, 1986, when he was notified of his son David's death due to the irresponsible act of a drunk driver.

As you read this book, you may weep, laugh, and rejoice, for within its pages Steve shares his joys and sorrows of life— as a child, a husband, a father, and as a minister of the gospel. Steve openly discusses the struggles he faced during the months and years that followed David's death, including anger, loneliness, despair, and even thoughts of suicide!

Tormented by the enemy of his soul with no hope for the future, Steve became "a miracle in the making" as he was rescued by the glorious love of Jesus Christ, the one and only hope for every tomorrow!

*Strength for Today, Bright Hope for Tomorrow* shares an inspirational message of hope, one that I have watched unfold in the life of my friend Steve Brock. As a recipient of God's abundant grace, he is committed to sharing this message of hope that he found in Jesus Christ with the hurting and the oppressed.

**Benny Hinn**
**January 1997**

# I Want
# to
# See Jesus

Shades of blue and amber lights danced slowly as a soft melody began to play. Swelling crescendos of music filled the auditorium, which was packed to capacity, as a rainbow of colored lights welcomed a dignified-looking man. His demeanor was confident, as though he didn't have a care in the world.

He walked slowly toward center stage, where he paused and planted his feet. With microphone in hand, the man pushed back his shoulders, took a deep breath, and began to sing these lyrics:

> *I dreamed of a city called glory,*
> *so bright and so fair,*
> *When I entered the gates, I cried holy,*
> *The angels all met me there. . . .*

His lilting tenor voice was pleasant to hear, and his style was smooth and crystal clear as he glided easily from note to note. As he sang the song, he delivered the familiar lyrics with precision, the words painting a serene picture of someone's first moments in heaven. Each syllable was pronounced with perfection and deep feeling, almost as if the words came straight from his own heart. As he continued to sing, his facial expressions revealed that he was becoming more and more enraptured with the song's message.

When he had successfully finished the first stanza, the music changed keys and ushered him easily into the second verse of the song. As he prepared to deliver the next stanza, he shifted noticeably from foot to foot, almost as if he were securing his stance. Then he stood still, stared deep into the audience, and began to sing the second verse:

> *As I entered the gates of that city,*
> *My son David, he knew me so well. . . .*

Midway, he lifted his head slightly and began to gaze upward. As he sang on, the message of the song seemed to carry him away from the crowd and the lights, beyond the walls of the auditorium. Although he continued to deliver the lyrics, it was almost as if he were being lifted into another realm that was beckoning to him.

> *He took me down the streets of heaven,*
> *Such scenes, too many to tell. . . .*

Then, for a brief moment, the singer paused. He stood motionless, seemingly unaware of his surroundings. Although thousands were seated before him in the crowded auditorium, he appeared to be unaware of their presence. His gaze was still fixed upward, and it seemed almost as if he were suspended somewhere between earth and heaven.

As the background music played on, he struggled to continue with the song. His face portrayed an inner battle of emotions; it seemed difficult for him to continue. His professionalism prevailed, however, and he forced himself to go on, delivering the words slowly and deliberately. He gazed heavenward while he sang, his gentle words filled with emotion and love. As he continued, there was a sense of wonder and anticipation in the arena's atmosphere. It was almost as if he could actually see what he was describing in song, and at any moment some veiled curtain would roll back to provide a glimpse of what his eyes were beholding for all those seated before him in the auditorium.

> *I saw Abraham, Isaac, and Jacob,*
> *Talked with Mark and Timothy. . . .*

Then came another pause as the singer struggled to communicate the remaining lyrics. With his eyes still transfixed on some invisible scene overhead, he swallowed hard, took a deep breath, and prepared to deliver the remaining words of the song. As he did, a tear escaped from the corner of his eye and trickled down his face. He wiped it away, only to have another take its place.

No explanation for the tears was needed, for the atmosphere was filled with love and expectation. The thousands seated before him were by now all active participants, experiencing the same emotions as the singer—brushing away a tear now and then, almost able to witness the same scene the gentleman on stage was beholding.

As tears of love streamed down the singer's beaming face, he stretched out his hand as if reaching into some unseen realm. He hesitated for just a moment as he struggled to regain his composure. His very countenance provided an inkling of the battle taking place within him.

Unsuccessful, he finally surrendered to the overwhelming emotion that was thundering through his being. As he wiped away the tears, his trembling voice spoke these broken words:

> *But I said, "David, . . ."*

Then another momentary pause, followed by the piercing delivery of these lyrics:

> *"I want to see Jesus."*

He sang the words at full volume, holding the final note of the phrase until he had no more air in his lungs to continue.

He paused once more, and as he prepared to communicate the closing line, the expression on his face changed. His tearstained face was now aglow with anticipation. Through his tears his eyes were crystal clear, and a blazing fire from somewhere deep within seemed to shine through his eyes, piercing the darkness of the arena.

Then with striking vocal perfection and every bit of strength he could gather, he sang the final phrase with intense volume for greater emphasis:

*He's the One Who died for me!*[1]

### Let Me Introduce You

The dignified man—Steve Brock.

The setting—the stage of a Benny Hinn Miracle Crusade.

The time—approximately ten years after the sudden and senseless death of his sixteen-year-old son David, who died as the result of an irresponsible act of a drunk driver.

To look at Steve now, one might never realize or be able to comprehend what trials and tests he has faced in the past. No noticeable signs of his loss are evident as he walks on stage. Microphone in hand, he appears confident, happy, and totally fulfilled as he prepares to sing.

But if one were able to lift the veil of yesterday, revealing the pain of the past that brought him to this place, one would be amazed at what valleys and struggles have preceded this moment.

Steve Brock has traversed the valley of sorrow that began on July 27, 1986, with just one telephone call. He has conquered the grief and depair that waged a war unlike any he had ever known. And he is living proof that it is possible to overcome such foes. The victory was not easy, and it came gradually—sometimes moment by moment, sometimes day by day—but it did come!

What was it that brought Steve Brock from the depths of sorrow and despair and gave him the courage to go on? In the midst of indescribable loss and great tragedy, what gave him the power to carry on? What is his secret? How did he find strength for today, and what gave him bright hope for tomorrow?

## CHAPTER 1

# THE UNFORGETTABLE TELEPHONE CALL

## THIS CAN'T BE REAL

*C* ould this be a dream?

*Impossible,* I mused. *David gone? . . . No . . . Surely, this can't be real. . . . This kind of thing always happens to other people. . . . It can't be happening to me!*

These thoughts and so many more filled my mind as I sat there in Pastor May's home trying to collect my thoughts. Although there were other people in the room, the deafening silence that seemed to surround me provided a perfect environment for the arguments that were going on in my mind. Tragedies only happen on television and to people you seldom know. They're not supposed to happen to you! My mind was filled with so many thoughts, and I was struggling to sort everything out.

It was Sunday, July 27, 1986, and I was preaching in Cartersville, Georgia, for the weekend at Pastor Danny May's church. Cartersville was on the way to Atlanta, the city that had been selected to host the biannual conference of the ministerial fellowship with which I had been associated for many years. The conference was an uplifting and inspiring time and it provided a great opportunity for me to see many of my longtime friends who were also in ministry. Our busy schedules and ministry responsibilities never seemed to allow enough time to stay in touch. The conference was the perfect setting for catching up on the past and touching base with old friends and acquaintances.

Although I often traveled alone for my speaking engagements, occasionally one of my sons would join me for the weekend. Tony, my older son, had gone with me this time. Pat, my wife, and David, our younger son, had stayed home and were planning to join Tony and me at the conference in Atlanta in a few days.

Pat and David had remained at home because of David's schedule. He was looking forward to the upcoming school year because he had been selected to be on the football team. Although we had previously lived in Hamilton, Ohio, for four years while I pastored the church there, we had moved away for several years and had just returned to the area within the last six months. It was late July, and even though school was out, football practice was already beginning. David was so excited about his new high school and being on the team that he insisted on staying home with Mom so he could take part in the orientation and practice sessions. Pat was planning to join me on Monday, and David was scheduled to fly to Atlanta the following weekend, after a week of intense football practice.

Tony and I had driven to Cartersville on Saturday. We left about three o'clock in the afternoon, after a game of golf with David. The three of us had a great time together as we always did. Playing golf with my boys was a pure delight for me. We all thoroughly enjoyed the game, and being outside in the beautiful summer sunshine made it perfect.

Throughout the golf game David was bubbling with excitement about football and the upcoming year in high school, and his never-ending comments on the subject only underscored his enthusiasm. You see, David was always the "noise" in our house, and his unceasing, happy chatter on a variety of topics was very familiar to the whole family. He always had something to say, no matter what the topic of conversation, and with school just around the corner, he was filled with excitement (and conversation) about what he felt the upcoming year held for him. And besides his excitement about the approaching school year, he was also proud of the fact that he was now a licensed driver, having finally passed his driver's test on Thursday of that week—just two days prior to our golf game. He had celebrated his sixteenth birthday a few months earlier on February 1 but had never gotten around to getting his license. After a great deal of encouragement (perhaps even some prodding from me), he had finally taken the driver's test and passed.

The weekend in Cartersville had been great, and Tony and I made the most of our time together. From the time we left home on Saturday afternoon, we had shared so much: an exciting baseball game on the radio as we drove to Cartersville, the services at the church on Sunday, and all the time in between. I cherished special times like these with my boys and tried to take Tony or David with me as often as possible. Even though the weekend had been short, Tony and I really had a wonderful time together.

Following a dynamic service on Sunday evening, Tony and I were invited to Pastor May's home for a time of fellowship. With two fabulous services behind us, I was looking forward to spending some time with my friend Pastor May.

## THE UNFORGETTABLE CALL

We had just begun to relax in the warmth of his home and enjoy some refreshments when the telephone rang. Our host excused himself and left the room to answer the call. At the time the telephone rang, I really didn't think much about it. After all, I had been a pastor-evangelist for years, and as a veteran of the ministry I knew that telephone calls at all hours of the day and night were synonymous with life in the parsonage.

Nothing seemed out of the ordinary until my friend Pastor May reappeared after a brief conversation on the phone. As he stepped slowly into the room, I noticed that the expression on his face had changed. When he left the room moments before to answer the telephone, he had been engaged in casual conversation punctuated with light laughter. Now he was silent, and his facial expression was sober and unusually serious.

He walked slowly toward me, weaving his way through the furnishings in the room. His fixed gaze held me captive as he continued to approach. As he planted his foot next to the chair where I was seated, he stopped for just a moment and glanced quickly at Tony, who was seated on the couch to my left. Then he stooped down slowly and knelt before my chair. He looked me straight in the eyes and forced out these words that would change my life forever: "Steve . . . something has happened at home."

I looked at him with an inquiring glance and said, "What happened?"

"Steve," he responded with noticeable anguish in his voice. "Something serious has happened. It's David."

"Oh my, what bone has he broken now?" I asked lightheartedly. David was notorious for getting hurt somehow. He was always breaking a bone or getting injured. In fact, his accidents and minor mishaps had become so common that they had almost become a family joke.

Danny May's piercing look continued, and his facial expression grew more somber. "It's very serious, Steve," he repeated. The tone of his voice was guarded and deliberate as he slowly forced out these words: "There's been a terrible car wreck . . . David is dead!"

I stared at him in silent disbelief. I had heard his words, but they didn't really register. *Impossible! David . . . dead? It can't be! There must be some mistake!* We had just said good-bye the preceding afternoon following our golf game. I turned to look at Tony. The look on his face was one of shock and utter dismay. "Dad, it can't be . . ." he blurted out. "Not my brother!"

I looked back at Danny's face. I couldn't believe what I had just heard. My eyes searched his face for some sign that would change the meaning of the words he had just spoken. "Danny, please . . . for God's sake, don't tell me that," I begged. "Please, please don't tell me that . . ." But the expression on Pastor May's face was somber and ever so serious. And the silence in the room was deafening. Even though I couldn't comprehend the words he had just spoken, his grave expression emphasized the seriousness of the moment.

My eyes darted quickly from one face to another, first to Tony . . . then back to Danny May . . . then back to Tony again. Tony just sat there in horrified disbelief, saying nothing. In fact, no one said anything. The moment was staggering, so much so that it's difficult to put into words the feeling that surged through my body. The silence that seemed to last forever confirmed the unbelievable news—David was dead!

## WHAT ABOUT PAT?

"I've got to call Pat," I said to Danny in a stupor. "I've got to talk to her." I pulled myself up out of the chair and walked toward the telephone, stunned and numb with pain.

I dialed the familiar number and waited for my wife to answer. "Hello?" she answered. Her voice was hesitant and uncertain.

"Pat, this is Steve . . . Pat . . . honey . . . please tell me it's not true . . ." My voice faded away as I waited for my wife to reassure me that this was all just a terrible nightmare. However, that reassurance never came.

"It's true, Steve . . . it's true . . ." she said, her words broken and drawn out. There was such pain in her voice as she spoke the words.

"No, Pat, no . . . not David," I said as I began to weep. "It can't be true . . . Patty . . . how can it be?"

"Steve," she answered slowly, "it really happened, and he's gone." Then there was silence. I could hear Pat crying softly on the other end of the telephone line. I can't describe the pain that I sensed in her voice as she spoke, and I was going through my own kind of agony on the other end of the line. I was at a loss for words; I didn't know what to say. I wanted to be with her to comfort her, but I was several hundred miles away from home. Not knowing what to say, I just waited for a moment.

Finally I managed to pull myself together enough to speak. "Well, I'll be home soon. Tony and I will catch the first plane available. I'll see you as soon as possible." I hung up the telephone and walked slowly back to the chair in which I had been sitting when the phone call came. As I sank into the chair, my thoughts carried me away from Pastor May's home to a dark, empty world I had never known.

## SUSPENDED IN TIME

I felt suspended in time as my mind raced a thousand miles a second to grasp what had happened. The shocking news drew me away from the warmth of the Mays' living room into the gloomy shadows of distress and loneliness.

The grief I felt was unbearable. I had experienced pain in many different ways throughout my life, beginning with the loss of my father when I was only two years old. But I had never known anything like this.

After my father died, my brother and I became very close, but even that relationship eventually became a source of pain. My brother and I had begun in the ministry together as teenagers, preaching and singing together. As adults we were close, and our families shared many wonderful experiences and memories. But because of a prescription drug problem, my brother had left the ministry, and our shared lives and goals were torn apart. All this had added a great deal of suffering to my life. I had struggled from time to time with the loss of my father and the relationship I had once shared with my brother.

But no disappointment or tragedy from my past could even come close to the pain I felt at that moment.

## RECOGNIZING THE ENEMY

In the midst of this terrible agony that ripped at my heart, the enemy of my soul came to steal and destroy, just as the Word of God states. "The thief does not come except to steal, and to kill, and to destroy. I have come that they may have life, and that they may have it more abundantly" (John 10:10).

At the height of this suffering and loss—some of the darkest hours of my life—the devil taunted and harassed my mind with these words: "This time you won't climb this mountain. I've got you this time! You'll never preach another gospel message or sing another gospel song. I've got you . . . you're finished!" The words tore at me, playing over and over in my mind.

I don't know how much time passed as I sat there, but eventually the background noise around me diminished, and the Mays' house grew silent. In the empty silence I sat alone, facing the cold dismal night ahead.

## THE LONGEST NIGHT

Despair and agony filled the long, lonely hours that followed. The darkness of night seemed to hold me captive for an eternity. I felt as if my heart had been ripped from my chest, and nothing brought me any relief from the agony and torment I felt. "Oh, God, not my boy, David," I cried over and over as I wrestled with the glaring reality.

My mind played tricks on me as the longest night of my life closed in around me. Time stood still as I tried to distinguish between what was real and what was not. In the cold emptiness of the midnight hours, the words rang over and over in my ears: "There's been a terrible car crash . . . David's dead!" I felt emotionally numb and yet besieged with relentless pain at the same time. Nothing subdued the raging tempest within.

Over the course of my thirty years in ministry as a pastor-evangelist, I had shared many crisis situations with individuals and members of my congregation. I had spent so many hours sitting with mothers and fathers in hospital waiting rooms, quoting verses of comfort and consolation from the Bible to help sustain them as they waited for news regarding a son or daughter.

On other occasions I had rushed to the side of a grieving parent after receiving news of some family tragedy. And in every situation, Scriptures of assurance and hope had poured from my lips with loving concern as I reminded them of God's love and grace toward them.

I thought back to a time nine years earlier when as a pastor I had attempted to comfort a mother and father in my congregation. Their seven-year-old son had suffered a severe head injury, and after lingering between life and death for three days, had been taken from them by death's cold grasp. My own son David was also seven years old at that time, and I still had vivid memories of how tightly I had hugged my seven-year-old son following that funeral service as I thanked God for him.

Now it was different. This time *I* was the father who was engulfed by the cloud of grief, and it was *my* son who had been snatched away in death. And in the darkness of the night I felt so alone . . . more alone than I had ever felt. None of the Scriptures I had quoted so many times to others in similar circumstances came to mind. Nothing was automatic now, and nothing seemed to help. I was empty, and I was drowning in a sea of sorrow. I was so alone. "Why, God?" I cried over and over. "Why my boy David?"

## WHY, GOD?

My questions of why rang over and over in my mind. *Why my boy? . . . Why David? . . . Why our family? . . . We've always lived for You, God . . . We've always served You . . . Why us? . . . Why did this happen?* My questions were endless. But no answers came. Nothing brought me any consolation as I drifted through the long, lonely hours of night.

I didn't realize it at the time, but I eventually learned that much of the trauma and emotion I experienced following the news of David's death was normal, according to MADD (Mothers Against Drunk Driving), an organization that reaches out to the survivors of drunk driver–related tragedies. They say that "immediately after the death of a loved one, especially if the death was sudden and violent, many people withdraw psychologically. Retreating is a healthy coping mechanism to manage pain and anxiety. Typical retreat strategies include shock, disbelief, numbness, confusion, disorientation, and denial."[1]

I experienced nearly all of these feelings during that first long, dark night on July 27, 1986: the numbness, the disbelief, the denial. And nothing provided the comfort that I so desperately sought.

## AT HOME IN HAMILTON

There's really no good way for such earth-shattering news to be delivered, for no matter how carefully it is handled, the result is the same: someone you love is gone forever!

When the telephone call came, Pastor May was so gentle in giving Tony and me the terrible news about David. But Pat learned what happened to David under very different circumstances.

She was at home all alone, packing and preparing for the conference in Atlanta. She had spoken to David at about 10:00 P.M. by telephone following the Sunday evening service at church, and everything was fine. He had phoned to check in and ask permission to go over to a friend's house from church to watch a video. David was always conscientious about staying in touch with his mother and me and kept us well informed as to his whereabouts.

Not long after her brief conversation with him, she stepped outside our back door for a breath of fresh air and saw two or three of our neighbors walking past the house. The neighborhood was very friendly, and everyone knew one another. After a friendly "Hello," they coaxed her into taking a walk with them around the neighborhood. The evenings were lovely at this time of year, so Pat agreed.

They had barely started walking when a policeman drove up to the house and pulled into our driveway. A number of officers lived in the neighborhood, so police cars were a common sight. Pat and the neighbors paused to find out why the policeman had stopped.

The officer got out of his car and said, "Can you tell me where the Brocks live? I'm trying to find the Brocks' house. It's very important that I locate them."

"Yes, sir, this is where the Brocks live. I'm Pat Brock," Pat responded.

"Is Mr. Brock here?" the officer asked.

"No, he and my son are in Georgia holding a meeting this weekend," Pat answered.

Pat, being a minister's wife, was accustomed to officers coming to our home. On many occasions when I was a pastor, it was quite common for the police to contact us at home before notifying someone regarding a crisis.

When the policeman realized that Pat was home alone, he said that there must be some mistake and apologized for disturbing Pat. Then he excused himself, got back into his car, and left quickly.

As he pulled out of the driveway, Pat and the neighbors decided to continue their walk around the block and strolled slowly away, dismissing the officer's visit. A few minutes later as they were walking along, talking about nothing in particular, Pat heard someone call her name from the street. When she looked to see who it was, she saw her friend Charlene Smith, who lived only a few blocks away. Pat walked over to Charlene's car to find out what Charlene was doing driving around the neighborhood at that time of night.

"Hey, Charlene, what are you doing here?" Pat inquired.

"I've been driving around, looking for you, Pat," Charlene said. "There's been a car crash, and David was involved somehow. We need to go to the hospital."

"Is David OK?" Pat asked.

"I think so," Charlene responded, "but I don't know any of the details. I got a call from a friend who didn't know any details except that David was in a wreck. I left the house immediately and have been looking for you. Let's go."

## WHERE'S DAVID?

The drive to the hospital took only a few minutes as it was only four or five blocks away from our house. Pat and Charlene arrived around 10:30 P.M. Pat got out of the car quickly and hurried toward the emergency room door. As she made her way down the hallway toward the waiting room, she was surprised to see a number of people from the church there. As she entered the waiting room, she was even more startled to see that area filled with many familiar faces too. The hallway, the waiting room, and eventually the parking lot were all jammed with people from the church—perhaps two to three hundred people in all. The buzz of the simultaneous conversations created a hum in the air of the waiting room.

As soon as Pat arrived she tried to find out something about David, but no one could really tell her anything. The emergency room staff were rushing around, obviously busy with their responsibilities. From time to time an update on the condition of a young female patient was reported by a member of the emergency room staff. What Pat would later discover was that the young girl whose condition was being discussed had been a passenger in David's car. Unaware of this, Pat paid little attention to that information. She assumed that some of the staff were also working with David, so she didn't press the issue. Anxious and concerned, she continued to wait for news of his condition.

Time dragged on, and she still had no news. As she waited,

her anxiety increased, and she became more concerned. Pat glanced at her watch. She had already been there an hour or more, and still there was no news on David's condition. She looked in the direction of the admissions area in the waiting room. She couldn't understand why no one had told her anything yet. At one point she looked back toward the admissions desk and noticed that Elizabeth Amburgey had just arrived. Elizabeth was a dear friend to Pat and me. We had worked closely with her when we pastored the church. She had been the Christian education director during my tenure as pastor and had continued to serve in that position. Pat and I had really come to love and appreciate her. In the uncertainty of this situation, Pat was relieved to see her there.

Elizabeth made her way through the crowded waiting area. She greeted Pat and Charlene with a loving hug and said, "I heard about the accident on the eleven o'clock news. I came straight to the hospital. How's David?"

"There's still no news," Pat answered. "I wish they would tell me something. What is taking so long?" Her voice revealed how worried she was.

The longer Pat waited, the more concerned she became. Soon the minutes turned into an hour, and an hour turned into two, and Pat still had received no information about David's condition.

Meanwhile the steady stream of people from church continued. Familiar faces were everywhere. There were several teenagers present, many of whom were David's close friends from the youth group, as well as a number of parents and adults too. The faces that filled the waiting room were all serious and showed marked concern—victims in some way or another of the uncertainty of the car wreck.

Years later I read something that I had never really thought about. The article said,

> In almost every drunk driving crash, there's still another group of victims, a group whose role as heroes often overshad-

ows their role as victims, but who suffer deeply from the consequences of drunk driving nonetheless.

They're the emergency personnel, police, firemen, rescue squad members, ambulance drivers, paramedics, physicians, emergency room attendants and more who, despite their incredible professionalism, never become hardened to the horrors they face.[2]

Pat recalls now that the marked concern of the police officer who came to the house to notify her of the car crash was apparent, especially if she had been looking for it. In retrospect she says the hospital personnel in the emergency room were also deeply and noticeably affected by the tragic circumstances. But at the time, she was so consumed with her own thoughts about David that their reactions didn't register with her.

As Pat nervously glanced around the crowded waiting room, she noticed more familiar faces, including Mike Medley and Jerry Flick. She was glad to see them there, especially since Tony and I weren't there with her. Mike and Jerry had begun attending the church during our four years there as pastor, and we had grown to love them and their families very much and had shared many good times together.

Mike and Jerry managed to inch their way through the crowded waiting area where Pat was waiting. By this time every hallway leading to the emergency room was overflowing with people from the church, and the waiting room was so crowded that they were standing shoulder to shoulder.

It was now about 1:15 A.M. and Pat had been waiting in the emergency room since about 10:30 P.M. Nearly two hundred people filled the crowded waiting room and were waiting anxiously for news of David. In the distance Pat heard a husky voice that cut through all the conversation and background noise. She looked in the direction from which the voice was coming to see an official-looking person talking to someone on the other side of the room. She later learned that he was the county coroner.

"Someone needs to identify the Brock boy," the thick voice said. "Where are the parents? They've got to identify the body."

The words cut to the core of her being. What was he saying? Stunned by the words, Pat glanced up to see Mike Medley walking toward her. He was only an arm's length away now, and she called out to him. "Mike, what is he saying? David . . . dead? . . . No, tell me it's not true! . . ." Her voice trailed off as she looked up at Mike for some words of comfort and hope.

By now the coroner was also walking in her direction, having discovered that she was David's mother. He stopped in front of her and said, "Ma'am, your boy is dead. You'll have to identify the body."

Still dazed by the words she had just heard, Pat looked up at Mike and then at Jerry, who were standing on her right and her left sides. Tears were rolling down her face as she stared into space trying to take in everything that was happening around her. Finally she mustered the strength to speak. Looking at the coroner she said, "Why didn't someone tell me something about David sooner? I've been waiting here for so long."

"Ma'am," the gentleman responded, "I just got here a little while ago. You see, legally, the hospital personnel could not advise you about your son's death until he was pronounced dead by someone from the coroner's office. Because the crash occurred on the driver's side of the car, it took some time to free him from the wreckage. After that, he was brought here and our office was contacted as is required by law. I need someone to make a positive identification now."

Pat turned toward Mike and Jerry and said, "Jerry, I can't . . . I just can't . . ."

"I'll identify the body for you if you like," Jerry offered. "I've already seen David because I came by the crash site shortly after it happened. Someone called me because they thought it might be my son in the car."

"I'll go with him," Mike said.

Pat just nodded her head in silent agreement as she wiped away the falling tears.

Jerry turned to the coroner and said, "I can identify him because I saw him at the scene of the crash. I can tell you that it's the Brock boy."

(While writing this book, I had occasion to speak with Jerry about some of the details of the night of the car crash. He told me that waiting there in that emergency room with Pat was the most difficult thing he had ever done. Our families had become so close, and we had shared so many happy times together. David and his son were great friends. David had even been part of the wedding party at Jerry's daughter's wedding.

That evening Jerry had originally received a telephone call about the wreck because someone thought his son, Walt, who resembled David considerably, might have been involved. He had rushed to the crash site facing the possibility that it might be Walt who had been injured. When he had arrived, however, he discovered that it was not his son, but David. During the hours that followed at the hospital, Jerry waited in silent agony. He felt the relief of knowing his son was all right, yet knowing that David was dead was sheer torment. And not knowing how to tell Pat had torn him apart inside as he waited with her for all those hours in the emergency room.)

Surrounded by people and stunned by the news, Pat just stood there, trying to absorb everything. As the coroner turned and walked away with Mike and Jerry, Pat was numb, unable to move. Elizabeth stood quietly by her side, waiting patiently. Elizabeth didn't know what to say, so she just put her hand on Pat's shoulder and waited until Pat was ready to go back home. Finally, some time after 1:30 A.M., Pat and Elizabeth slowly walked out of the emergency room and left the hospital to face the long night ahead.

## WHAT A NIGHTMARE

Back at the Mays' house the darkness that surrounded me in that room eventually gave way to the dawning of a new day as the sun rose. A sense of relief seized me for just a moment as the first rays of the morning sun crept into the room through the window. What a long night . . . what a terrible nightmare . . . or was it a nightmare?

I replayed the events of the previous evening in my mind, one detail at a time. Danny had reminded me that Patty was at home in Hamilton packing for the conference, preparing for her trip to Atlanta where she was to meet Tony and me. David had gone to church alone that evening, driving the familiar fifteen-minute route to the church by himself since he now had a driver's license.

Following the service, several of the high schoolers had gathered at their favorite restaurant. Then they had returned to the church parking lot to "hang out" as kids do. One of the teenagers suggested they get a video and get together at his home to watch it. David had called his mother at about 10:00 P.M. to tell her what the group was going to do and to ask her permission to drive to the home where the group was to assemble. Pat had answered, "Yes, but make sure you don't break curfew." (The reminder about curfew was only a formality because David was always a good kid—not the kind of boy who would break curfew—and Pat knew she could depend on him to be home on time.)

As David left the parking lot, he turned out of the church driveway and began to slowly accelerate on the familiar road in front of the church. Within seconds a drunk driver appeared from nowhere and came flying over the hill from the opposite direction. Although David was only traveling thirty to thirty-five miles an hour, the other driver had been going an estimated ninety miles an hour. Danny said the impact had been directly to the driver's side, and David had been killed instantly.

A few days later my brother-in-law, who is a licensed mortician by profession, confirmed that David had indeed been killed instantly. He said that because there was no bruising to David's body, it was apparent that he had died between heartbeats or instantly. The only visible sign of injury on David was a tiny cut near one eyebrow. In the midst of such tragic circumstances, there was a measure of comfort for Pat and me in knowing that David had slipped into eternity in this way.

I had gone over and over the sketchy details of the car crash throughout the long, lonely night. I was exhausted and emotionally spent, having slept very little. By this time I wasn't certain what was real and what was not. I asked myself the same questions again that I had considered as the warm morning sun announced the new day: *Have I just awakened from the worst nightmare of my life? Is this really happening to me? Is David really gone? Has his precious life really been snatched away by a drunk driver?*

As I sat motionless in the morning light, attempting to sort out the events of the previous night, a feeling of utter despair swept over me. I was not in any physical pain, yet I ached to the very core of my being. Something deep within me cried out for relief, but no help came. The more I thought about it, the more I hurt. I had never experienced such agony. As that pain from deep within surged through me, it grew in intensity, and I was slowly gripped with the awful realization that this terrible nightmare was not just a bad dream. It was a reality, and David was dead!

## GATE 4

I'll never forget my arrival at Gate 4 of the Cincinnati International Airport on July 28, 1986. Although Tony was at my side, I have never felt so alone in my life.

Tony and I got off the plane and began to walk down the hallway. In the distance I could see the silhouettes of my two friends Mike Medley and Jerry Flick, who had come to meet us. They were just standing there, motionless, waiting for us as we walked down the seemingly endless concourse toward the terminal.

When Tony and I finally reached the end of the long corridor, Mike and Jerry took a step toward us and reached out to embrace us. As they wrapped their strong arms around Tony and me, no words were necessary. They just held us, trying to comfort us as best they could.

I finally gathered the strength to speak, repeating the same words over and over to Mike and Jerry: "I just can't believe it . . . I just can't believe it's true . . . not David . . ." As I paused and looked into Jerry's face, he reluctantly offered an unsolicited response, "It's true, Steve; I've seen him."

I don't know how long we stood there, minutes perhaps. I had lost all awareness of time since the telephone call the night before. Mike and Jerry's love and concern for Tony and me were communicated in such a strong manner, even though very little was said. We just stood there, weeping together, sharing the pain.

So many times before I had gotten off the plane at Gate 4. Each time I did, I had a spring in my step and a sense of excitement, for I was always eager to get home to my wife and two sons. They were my life; they brought purpose and meaning to my existence; and I would always hurry to collect my baggage so I could get home to my family.

But today was different. Today this corridor was cold and empty; there was no joy or expectancy in me. Today there was no reason to hurry home, for now everything would be different. David wouldn't be there to run out and meet me as I drove into the driveway. He wouldn't be there to grab my suitcase and carry it into the house. There would be no report about the football practice and the team. David wouldn't be there this time— he was gone!

## ALONE IN A CROWD

Somehow Mike and Jerry got Tony and me out of the airport and into an automobile. I don't remember much about that, but I can recall looking out of the car window and seeing our house in the distance. As we drove up to the house, I noticed that there were cars everywhere. But why they were there was not important to me at the time. I had been lost in deep thought as we made our way from the airport to our home. Everywhere I looked, I saw something that reminded me of David. Everything reminded me of him, and my mind was filled with thoughts of him. As we drove by the golf course, my mind caught a brief glimpse of his face as I reflected on our golf game just two days earlier—realizing that this would never be again.

So much had changed in such a short time. Tony and I had just driven out of town two days before with so much to look forward to. We had listened to the Atlanta Braves game on the radio and marveled about how David was missing this for football practice. But now, what was left? I felt so alone, so empty. How could this be happening to our family? It had always been someone else before—never the Brocks! Not us!

Jerry pulled the car into the driveway and got out of the car to open the door for Tony and me. He and Mike walked with us as we entered the house side by side.

Tender voices called my name in the distance as I walked aimlessly through the door. It seemed as though it took every ounce of energy I had within me just to take the next step. I don't think I responded to anyone's comments as I entered the house, but kept moving forward in an attempt to find a place to be alone.

As I walked on, I saw Pat standing there, surrounded by people. The house was crowded because so many people from the church had come to be with her while she waited for Tony and me to return. Tears began to flow freely down my face and fall to the floor as I walked over to her. She looked so weary and her eyes were filled with such sadness. I reached out to her, and we fell into each other's arms. We stood there, weeping, unable to speak.

That day our house was filled with sadness, and it seemed so empty, even though so many friends and acquaintances were there. Elizabeth Amburgey was there. She had stayed with Pat since the news of the tragedy came, even sleeping on the floor at the end of Pat's bed all night so she wouldn't be alone.

In the background I heard someone call my name again, but I ignored it and focused on Pat. I looked into my wife's tearstained face and said, "It can't be true . . . our baby boy . . . our David . . . gone?"

She nodded and said, "But it's true, Steve . . . he's gone." As she spoke the words, another tear rolled down her cheek.

We stood there, embracing one another. I was vaguely aware of the quiet conversation all around me, but only Pat mattered at that moment. I don't know how long we stood there trying to comfort each other, but I eventually took a step back and walked slowly away from Pat. There were people all around me, but I didn't take the time to identify the faces. I was glad they had been there for Pat, but at the moment I just wanted to be alone with my thoughts.

I found a chair away from the commotion and the people. As my body sank into the chair, I began to go over everything again, moment by moment. I sat there, motionless, as I tried to find my way through the blurred memories of the last twenty-four hours. I really don't know how long I sat there, mulling everything over, but I just couldn't stop thinking about it. Only days before I had felt as if I didn't have a care in the world, but now life seemed so fragile and uncertain. This day was so much different from any I had ever anticipated. What would tomorrow hold?

## CHAPTER 2

# SAYING
# GOOD-BYE

## THE EMPTY HOUSE

*T*he days following David's death were long and difficult ones. At times my mind would tell me, *This isn't really happening. You'll wake up and find out it's just a bad dream.*

I desperately wanted to believe that what was happening was just a bad dream, but each morning as I awoke, I discovered all too well just how real this tragedy was. The incessant emptiness that haunted every waking moment only echoed my great loss.

No matter what I did, nothing filled the aching void within me. Everywhere I turned there were reminders of David: the deafening silence in the house that had once been filled with David's cheerful voice; the noiseless stairway in the early morning where his footsteps had once announced his arrival; the unoccupied lounge chair on the sundeck under the warm July sun; his dark, empty room at the top of the stairs. Wherever I turned in our home, the glaring absence of David reminded me that he wasn't coming home.

His sudden and unexpected departure from life and from our home and family had left a far greater vacuum in our lives than an empty bedroom and silence. I was empty, and I felt as if every ounce of life had been drained out of me. In a moment's time so many of my hopes and dreams had evaporated along with all the plans related to David's future: David's aspirations to "minister with Dad when I grow up," the baseball games, discussing the latest cars, the golf games we once enjoyed sharing so much, high school graduation, talk of college and a career, and so much more.

During his short life of only sixteen years he had brought so much joy to Pat and me. He always had an uncanny ability to make us laugh and put everything in the proper light. As a person, he was a delight. He had so much to offer, and I know that he would have had a great impact on the world, if given the opportunity.

But everything about David and his potential to make the world a better place came to a screeching halt in a fraction of a second. The reckless deliberate decision of a teenager to drive while intoxicated served as the mechanism that stole David's life away, impacting Pat and me along with so many others. A head-on collision had killed him instantly, and in just a moment, our world was turned upside down, never to be the same.

With the dawning of each new day, I was becoming increasingly aware that there was no way to go back to the way things used to be. The pain I felt deep within was relentless, never subsiding. As one day blended into the next, the pain grew worse and more intense. It was all-consuming, and all I thought about was what I had lost: David. I focused on my loss and forgot about everything else. I felt as if my life had ended—and it almost had.

## AM I SEEING THINGS?

A day or two after David's death as I sat alone in an empty room in our house, I was startled by a noise and a shadowy figure rounding the corner of the adjoining room. From my favorite chair I stared at the silhouette in disbelief. My eyes were transfixed on a dark-haired image with curly hair, which quickly vanished around the corner. The build, the hair—I couldn't believe my eyes! I rose up out of my chair and stood there motionless, looking in the direction of the disappearing image. "My God," I cried out in utter relief. "It isn't real after all! . . . David, is that you?"

As the question left my lips, my son Tony's wet head appeared from around the corner. He had just showered and was on his way to his room. "Dad, are you all right?" he asked hesitantly.

His familiar voice startled me. I blinked my eyes a couple of times as I looked at him and managed to mumble an affirmative answer. Satisfied, he turned around and left just as quickly as he had appeared.

I couldn't believe it. For just a fraction of a second, I thought it was David. But then it couldn't be—he was gone forever!

## DIFFICULT DECISIONS

Confronting the reality of the situation and dealing with the wide range of emotions that accompanied our tragic loss were some of the most difficult things with which we had to cope. And in the midst of our painful memories and incessant grief, Pat and I were faced with decisions on a daily basis—decisions that come with the death of a loved one: notifying friends and relatives, selecting a casket, choosing the burial clothes from the neatly hung garments in the closet of the empty bedroom, the funeral service, the flowers, the final resting place, and so many other details. Our family and friends tried to help, but many of the decisions could only be made by us.

I still remember how difficult our meeting with the funeral director was. Having previously served as a pastor in that city, I had become acquainted with him on a professional basis. I had officiated at a number of memorial services where he had handled the details of the funeral. Now, however, my contact with him was on a personal basis, and I was the one who had lost a loved one. Although he was very helpful during this painful process, the entire encounter only reaffirmed our loss. There was no way to insulate us from the painful reality. Each decision served as a glaring reminder of the finality of what had happened. David was gone.

Our dear friends Virgil and Elizabeth Amburgey were a tremendous blessing to us during this time. If it hadn't been for them, I don't know if we would have made it through those days of grief and pain. As I mentioned before, Elizabeth had stayed with Pat the night of the wreck while Tony and I were in Cartersville. Her love and concern for Pat were evidenced as she slept on the floor at the foot of Pat's bed throughout the night, just in case Pat needed her.

Both she and her husband were there for us, day after day, as we grieved and prepared to say good-bye to David. They were there for us, always ready to help with whatever we needed, yet sensitive enough to allow us the necessary privacy to mourn our loss. Even when we didn't need anything, they were still there, loving us and supporting us in our sorrow. Their friendship and love rang clear and strong and cut through the overpowering silence that now filled our home. And their tenderness sustained us when well-meaning people made attempts to comfort us that were anything but consoling.

## AN ATTEMPT AT COMFORT

Until we lost David, I never realized how the comments and actions of some individuals can affect you. Unless you have experienced the loss of a child or close loved one, it's difficult to know what a grieving family goes through. There are no right words to say—nothing that will distract you or ever make you forget what has happened.

During those days immediately following the car wreck, many well-intentioned individuals tried to comfort us in a variety of ways. Some became very religious and endeavored to offer an explanation on God's behalf about what happened. Others quoted Scripture and attempted to add some spiritual statement of sympathy or condolence. A few were relentless in trying to get me to talk about the tragedy. Although I'm sure that each one meant well, this was not at all what Pat and I wanted to hear. In fact, it almost produced feelings of resentment toward many who were nothing more than mere acquaintances. I found myself wanting to shut them out and get away.

At a time of tragedy and personal loss such as this, you really don't know how to feel. I internalized much of the pain I was feeling. I really didn't want to talk about it because I was still trying to sort everything out. Virgil and Elizabeth Amburgey allowed me that privilege. They were very discerning and considerate of me, unlike some of the well-intentioned individuals who pressed me with questions. Because I was hurting so badly, I couldn't bring myself to discuss David's death. Then when someone whom you really don't know seems to demand a response, it becomes an impossible situation. Manners go out the window, and you want to push them away and be left alone with your pain and fading memories.

Pat and I soon became like closed flowers, unwilling to open up about what we were feeling deep inside. At the height of our grief Elizabeth and Virgil, along with a handful of very special friends, were there for us. Their silent strength and constant love helped to carry us through those dark days of decision making.

We eventually made the decisions and finalized all the details for David's memorial service. During those days I shed so many tears that I felt certain I could not cry any more. But each time the memories, the sadness, or any reminder of David surfaced, a river of tears would pour out of me once again, almost as if to wash away some of the pain.

## HIS GRACE IS SUFFICIENT

As I look back on those dark days now, I realize just how much God sustained us. It's also clear to me now how God's grace was with us, even though we didn't always recognize it at the time it was manifest. Since childhood I was taught that God's grace is always sufficient to carry you through any circumstance. Although I had never had any doubts about this teaching, I personally had never faced a situation that truly affirmed this.

However, in my greatest hour of need, I experienced the reality of 2 Corinthians 12:9, which says, "My grace is sufficient for you, for My strength is made perfect in weakness." This was God's assurance to Paul that His grace would sustain him in his hour of trial, and that he could depend wholly upon the power of God to carry him through any circumstance. Like Paul, I experienced this measure of grace during the days that surrounded David's untimely death and in the weeks and months that followed. Although that grace did not come early, it was available at the moment of my need and sustained me in my weakest hours.

Recently while reading a book titled *Christ the Healer* by F. F. Bosworth, I read something in a section titled "Paul's Sufferings" that provided some wonderful insights for me. I happened to read these paragraphs just days before the tenth anniversary of David's death, and I was reminded once again of how God has showered His grace upon my life day by day:

> Soon after Paul's conversion, God said to Ananias, "I will show him how great things he must suffer for My name's sake," not by sickness, but by the persecutions which Paul enumerates as his buffetings. Paul had persecuted the Christians from place to place, and now he, himself, was beginning to experience the same and greater persecutions. Specifying the buffetings instigated by Satan's angel, Paul goes on to say, "Therefore I take pleasure in infirmities, in reproaches, in necessities, in persecutions, in distresses for Christ's sake; for when I am weak then am I strong." Paul first mentions "infirmities," for he realized, and every Christian should realize, his weakness and inability in his own strength to stand up against a satanic messenger, and to pass triumphantly through "reproaches, necessities, persecutions, distresses," and all the other buffetings he elsewhere catalogues; and this is why he besought the Lord three times to be rid of *him* (the messenger) who was buffeting him so severely

and in so many ways. Christ responded to his thrice-repeated prayer, not by removing the satanic messenger, but by saying, "My grace [which is for the "inner" man] is sufficient for thee; for My strength is made perfect in weakness."[1]

Paul's thorn was permanent, just as the loss of a loved one is permanent. God said, "My grace is sufficient." God's grace was sufficient for Paul, and it is sufficient for you and me. Bosworth went on to say:

When Paul saw that the grace of God was sufficient to strengthen him to bear all these things, he exclaimed, "Therefore will I rather glory in my infirmities [weaknesses] that the power of Christ may rest upon me . . . for when I am weak then am I strong."[2]

In my opinion, the word *therefore* is a word that means "affirmation without question." I believe Bosworth affirms this as he continues with:

How could it be true that Christ's strength was made perfect in Paul's weakness if he was left weak, or unless Paul was an actual partaker of Christ's strength, which would remove the weakness, whether it was physical or spiritual? Without God's strength being imparted to him is a man powerful when he is weak, either physically or spiritually? Paul saw that the grace of God given him made his very buffetings, even his imprisonments, to work together for his good and to turn out for the "furtherance of the Gospel." What servant of God has not learned, and probably more than once, that it is when he is most conscious of his own weakness that the power of Christ rests upon him the most; or, that it is when he is consciously weakest in himself that he is the strongest because of depending, not on his own, but on Divine strength?[3]

All things don't always happen as you would like, but as Scripture declares, "We know that all things work together for good to those who love God, to those who are the called according to

His purpose" (Romans 8:28). In other words, all things don't always work, but all things will work together for good to those who love God if we just give the situation to Him.

The grace that Paul referred to was for spiritual and not physical infirmities. Bosworth went on to say, "Paul is clear in teaching that it is the '*Life* of Jesus' which is 'made manifest in our mortal flesh,' but it is nowhere stated in the Scriptures that God gives *grace* to our *bodies*. The very word 'grace' shows that it was the 'inner man' that needed help, because the grace of God is imparted only to the 'inner man,' which Paul says, in his case, was 'renewed day by day.'"[4] There were no leftovers. And just as God provided manna for the children of Israel day by day, specifically providing for their needs, so He, too, provides grace sufficient to carry you and me through each day.

## GRACE TO CARRY ME THROUGH

I think one of the first times I was really aware of God's grace during the days that followed David's death was on the day of the funeral. I can remember it almost as though it were yesterday.

Pat, Tony, and I had gone by the funeral home to say our last good-byes to David before going to the church for the memorial service. As we walked into that room and saw David, we just stood there silently looking at him. Although the only visible injury was the tiny cut on his forehead as I mentioned before, seeing his lifeless body lying there before us had a very sobering effect. My heart was filled with both love and pain at that moment—I couldn't speak. Pat and Tony just stood there beside me, gazing at David, saying nothing.

I don't know how long we stood there, motionless—in the silence—several minutes, I suppose. Finally, we each took a moment to privately say our good-byes in our own way. I can remember watching Tony place a carefully folded note that he had written in the casket. I watched as Pat leaned over David's body, gently placed her hand on his hair, straightened his tie as she had done so many times when he was alive, and whispered something. Having completed her last motherly act for David, she paused just long enough to place a note in the casket too. Then she slowly began to move away from the casket. As she stepped back, she glanced in my direction with tear-filled eyes, suggesting it was now my turn to say good-bye to David.

I slowly approached the casket that held the lifeless body of my son. In this brief moment so many thoughts raced through my mind. How could I begin to put into words all that my heart held for my boy? I stood there beside the casket for a moment, gazing at David's handsome face. I was in no hurry to say a final good-bye to him. We had shared so much, and I missed him so. Filled with love, I finally leaned forward and placed a note that I had written in advance beside David. I've chosen not to share the contents of that note, for the words that I penned on that tearstained page are personal. As I looked at David lying there in that casket, tears rolled down my face and my heart whispered, "I love you, David."

Leaving David there was difficult. It was all so final that I just couldn't leave. Two of my dear friends, Gene Rice and C. R. Spain, were there, too, and they were a great strength to me. Gene was like a big brother to me, and I had known him for years. We were such close friends; we had prayed together on many occasions and had also ministered together. C. R. Spain was like the father I had never known. You see, my father had died when I was quite young, and until C. R. Spain came into my life, I had no real father image that I could look to. Like a father, he had been there for me when I needed him in the past, and on that day I needed his love and strength more than ever.

I can remember Gene and C. R. wrapping their arms around me and saying, "Come on, Steve, it's time to go." Pat and Tony had been waiting quietly several steps away from David's casket. As Gene and C. R. gently reminded me of the time, Pat turned and began to walk toward the door slowly. Tony followed close behind. I tried to move, but I couldn't. I couldn't bring myself to leave David. Gene and C. R. waited patiently as I stood there, unable (or perhaps unwilling) to move. Finally they began to slowly turn toward the door as their arms tightened around me. "Come on, Steve," they repeated as they took another step.

Nudged along by the motion of their bodies, I began to move slowly toward the door, keeping my eyes on David as I stepped reluctantly away from the casket. As I moved toward the exit, I can remember looking over my shoulder. I didn't want to take my eyes off David. Gene and C. R. stayed close beside me as I took one step and then another. I continued to look over my shoulder as I walked out of the room. I fastened my eyes on David and kept looking at him as long as I could. Finally, the wall got in the way, and I couldn't see him anymore. I held on to David as long as I could. And God's grace sustained me as I said my final good-bye to him. God's grace helped me do something I could never have done on my own.

As you read these pages you may be thinking, *I could never do that. I wouldn't have the strength.* But you can do whatever is necessary in life if God gives you the grace, the strength, and the ability, for God's Word promises, "My grace is sufficient for you, for My strength is made perfect in weakness" (2 Corinthians 12:9). God's grace is available to you at all times but is most apparent and most needed when you are at your weakest point. At that moment, His grace will be perfect to sustain and strengthen you if you will call upon Him.

## TEN YEARS LATER

Even though it has been ten years since David's death, I have found that God's grace is still sufficient for me on a daily basis. The same measure of grace that brought the strength and understanding necessary to carry me through this tragedy also sustains me today. As a born-again believer, I have a hope that goes beyond the grave. Second Corinthians 5:1 states in *The Living Bible*, "For we know that when this tent we live in now is taken down—when we die and leave these bodies—

we will have wonderful new bodies in heaven, homes that will be ours forevermore, made for us by God himself, and not by human hands."

Although David's departure was premature, and we are presently separated, there will come a day when I will be reunited with him to rejoice eternally. It is that grace that at times bursts into my spirit, bathing me with a hope that acknowledges that although he's gone, it's not forever. As F. F. Bosworth said, "God has never promised to take away from Christians their *external* buffetings *(repeated blows)*, afflictions and temptations; he gives us grace to bear them."[5]

## THE FAREWELL SERVICE

A short drive from the funeral home took us to the church where the memorial service was to be held. We arrived just before the service was to begin, pausing in the foyer briefly before entering the sanctuary. Although I had once served as pastor of this church and had spent innumerable hours within its walls, today it seemed like a foreign place.

The music began, signaling that the memorial service was beginning. My body seemed to be almost paralyzed with grief as I stood there. I didn't know if I would be able to move or go on. At about that moment I felt someone move toward me and stop beside me. When I looked to my left and my right, I discovered that I was standing between Pat and Tony. I took a deep breath as someone stepped forward to push open the double doors to the sanctuary.

I could hear the choir singing a beautiful song by Greg Nelson and Gary McSpadden titled "Jesus Lord to Me." Pat and I had selected it because of the lyrics.

> *If I had seen the sunset on the day that Jesus died,*
> *and felt the glow of the sunrise when the tomb was opened wide;*
> *Would I have known You, could I have seen*
> *that You were more than just a man, You were Lord and King.*
> *But now I know You, and I can see*

*That You are Lord of all, and You are Lord to me.*
*Jesus, Jesus, Lord to me;*
*Master, Savior, Prince of Peace;*
*Ruler of my heart today,*
*Jesus, Lord to me.*[6]

The music continued as the three of us stood there motion-less, clinging to one another. My eyes followed the long aisle that led to the front of the sanctuary. Although this church was quite familiar to me, today the aisle seemed much longer than I remembered. In the distance I could see the casket that cra-dled David's body. It all seemed so final and sad.

Tony and Pat were huddled close to me, and I felt their bod-ies take a step forward. I didn't think I could move. My legs felt weak, and my feet felt as if they were encased in cement. They were so heavy I didn't know if I could even take a step. It was almost as if I couldn't even remember how to walk.

Pat and Tony glanced at each other quickly, and their eyes seemed to ask the same question: "Will Dad make it?" They moved closer to me, held on tighter, and took another step. A war of emotions was raging within me, and I felt as if I were being torn apart inside. Having them close somehow helped to strengthen me. Slowly, I lifted one foot, and then the other, tak-ing one step at a time. I wept almost uncontrollably as I inched my way down the aisle. Somehow part of me still couldn't believe this was happening, yet the surroundings were undeniable. It must be real because there we were—Pat, Tony, and me—hud-dled close together, slowly making our way down the aisle of the church toward the flowers, the casket, and David.

We finally completed what seemed like an endless journey down the aisle. One by one we took our seats on an empty pew at the front of the church. We settled into our seats and waited for the memorial service to continue. As the choir finished the song, I took a deep breath and tried to hold back my tears. It was so difficult, though, because there—right in front of us— was the casket that held David's body. It was all so final. Feeling some movement beside me, I turned my head slightly, only to see Pat reaching for something to dry her eyes with too. Tony's face was also tearstained.

I turned and glanced at the faces of those seated nearby. Many of them were young faces, friends of David's from both church and school. The entire football team, including the coach, was there too. Some of them had been close to David and were there today as his friends and also as pallbearers.

The church was filled with people, and there were flowers everywhere, representing how David had touched so many lives in his brief sixteen years of life. As I glanced toward the front again, my eyes stopped for a moment as I gazed at the casket that held the body of my precious David. No words escaped my lips, but from the depths of my being, I cried out, "Why David? That's my boy's body lying there . . . how I miss you, son . . . oh, how I miss you!"

As I sat there consumed with grief and loss, I heard the heavenly Father whisper these words of comfort to my heart—words that I will never forget: "Have no fear. I know how you feel. David is standing here beside Me with his hand in Mine. Steve, I know how you feel because I lost My Son too."

At that moment I realized that God's grace was sufficient for me in my hour of weakness; without His strength, it would have been impossible for me to cope with these circumstances. These words represented God's grace to me, for the greatest definition of grace I know of is God doing something for us that we cannot do for ourselves. There was absolutely no way I could have walked down that aisle or dealt with the loss of my son David. But God helped me do something that day that I could not have done in my own strength. He helped me to carry on.

## FRIENDS AND LOVING MEMORIES

Many of my closest friends were there for me that day, loving me and sharing my pain. Several of them participated in the memorial service. LaVerne Trip, a friend I had come to know and love through our shared experiences with Trinity Broadcasting Network, a Christian television network, had left a meeting early so he could be there to sing. C. R. Spain, my friend and a most eloquent preacher, was present to share some warm, loving words just before a group named CornerStone sang. CornerStone was a singing group made up of several teenagers, a group that David had been a member of. Having them there was very meaningful, but hearing them sing that day without David was a very emotional experience for me, too, because it provided another glaring reminder that David was gone.

My friend Gene Rice preached a dynamic message from the book of 1 Samuel. His text was taken from 1 Samuel 21:1, where Samuel said, "Then came David . . ." (KJV). His message continued on to the first verse of the following chapter, which says, "David therefore departed." He interjected many warm thoughts about how David had come into our lives, and also how he had departed. Although the service was as we had planned, it was very difficult and quite emotional.

Other dear friends like Paul Crouch, founder and president of Trinity Broadcasting Network, his wife, Jan, along with Matt and Lori Crouch, rearranged their schedules and came as quickly as possible. Paul and Jan stopped by on their way to New York. They arrived that afternoon and took time to visit the gravesite and to express their love and concern to Pat and me. Their presence there meant so much to me, more than words can tell.

Throughout this long, painful day God's grace carried me just as 1 Peter 5:10 says: "But may the God of all grace, who called us to His eternal glory by Christ Jesus, after you have suffered a while, perfect, establish, strengthen, and settle you."

I will be forever grateful to Dr. T. L. Osborn for a statement that he made to me following the funeral. He is a mighty man of God who has impacted the world on a massive scale for years with the message of God's love. His simple but profound statement to me was based upon his own personal experience when he and his wife, Daisy, lost a child in death whom they had loved dearly. He said, "As you heal others, God will heal you." He went on to tell me that after his son's funeral, he and his wife left for Africa where they experienced great breakthroughs in their ministry. He said, "Daisy and I did that because we thought the best thing for us was to get back into the ministry. We thought as we were able to heal others, God would heal us. And that is exactly what has happened."

## THE GREATEST VICTORY

Following the memorial service, we took the slow drive to the cemetery. David's car had been hit head-on only a few hundred feet from the church. Consequently, the route for the funeral procession passed right by the place where the car crash had occurred just days before. This was the first time I had been on that road since the tragedy. I couldn't hold back the tears as we drove slowly along, and the pain I felt was clearly evident.

I glanced at Pat and Tony as I wept. In that moment of grief, Tony made a statement that began my slow but steady journey to recovery. As I sat there weeping, Tony looked at me through his big, brown eyes and said, "Dad, this is not the place of David's greatest defeat. It's the place of David's greatest triumph because he went from here to eternity."

Tony's wise words of insight at that moment helped to pull me out of my despair, reminding me that I had to make it for my family's sake. I couldn't fail them!

Although this was only one day in the process of recovery, and many other days of despair occurred later, I began to realize that my life was not over. David would not have wanted me to throw away everything and quit, so for his sake, for my family's sake, and for the Lord's sake, I had to go on. I had to get better.

## A LOVING MEMORIAL

My memories of the memorial service and the short service that followed at the cemetery are vague. The waves of grief that rolled over me made me somewhat numb to everything. But although I don't recall in detail all the aspects of the memorial service or what was said as we stood at the graveside, I do remember with clarity the helpless feeling that welled up within me as the casket bearing David's precious body was lowered into the ground. Since David's birth up until that moment I had committed myself to protecting and caring for him. Pat and I had loved and nurtured him and watched him grow into a fine young man. He had been such a joy to us, and nothing had ever separated us. But now the separation seemed final. David was gone, and I had no choice about leaving David here in the Good Shepherd Garden, the section of the cemetery in which Pat and I had selected a gravesite for our son.

Walking away from David's grave that day was the most difficult thing I have ever done. Although the setting in the Good Shepherd Garden was tranquil and a beautiful statue of Jesus holding a lamb stood nearby, those steps that led away from David's final resting place that day were the most difficult ones I have ever taken.

The words of a Chinese proverb I once heard are a reflection of what I felt that day. The proverb says, "Great is the pain of he who lives beyond his children."

The pain I felt that day was not visible nor could it be alleviated by some pain remedy. It was the greatest level of pain and agony I have ever experienced.

Those footsteps away from David's grave that day were nearly impossible for me. They did not lead away from the pain or end the terrible tragedy that had consumed us since that telephone call came on July 27. Rather than carry me away from the grief, they took me to many lonely hours that became days and weeks . . . to more questions with no apparent answers . . . to shattered dreams . . . and to the threshold of a whole new, empty life without David.

## CHAPTER 3

# SHATTERED DREAMS

*H*ow many in your party, sir?" the hostess asked.

Although I had no appetite to speak of, Pat and Tony had convinced me that we should get out of the house and go to a restaurant for dinner. It had been only days since the funeral, and trying to eat at home was difficult. It just wasn't the same without David. With some reluctance, I had agreed to go to the restaurant for their sake.

"Excuse me, sir, how many in your party?" the hostess repeated.

Without thinking, I responded, "Four," as I always had. As soon as the word passed my lips, I was immediately gripped with the realization that our "four" had now become "three." I stared at the lady in silence for a moment. Then I began to weep as the pain welled up within me. Any appetite I had vanished as the tears flowed freely. The thought of facing that empty place at the table was more than I could bear. Through the tears I looked at Pat and Tony and said meekly, "Come on, I just can't do this," and walked out of the restaurant.

This type of thing happened time after time. Attempting to go on with life, we would do something we had done when David was still with us. And each time we were reminded in some way that our "four" had become "three." With each occurrence we were dealt another harsh reminder of how radically our lives had been changed—David was gone!

## WHERE DO WE GO FROM HERE?

With David's sudden and unexpected death, the door to the future was slammed shut, and all the dreams for his life were snatched away in a moment's time. In the weeks and months that followed, the sense of loss I felt only increased.

At first, I think I mourned the loss of David because I missed him so much, along with all the good times we had shared. I missed his laughter and the happy noise that he brought to our home. We had always had so much fun together, and he was a part of nearly all that happened at our house. I missed everything attached to his short life and everything we had shared.

But as time went on, I became familiar with a different kind of grief—a sense of loss for what never was and for what never would be. Now my sorrow was not just based upon losing David and everything we had enjoyed together; I suffered deep regret for everything that had been stolen from the future we would have shared. There was no way I would ever see him play in another football game. We would never share another game of golf. I would never see my David walk across a high school stage to receive his diploma. We would never minister together, as he so often talked about. I would never help him buy his first car or see him go off to college. I would never see him get married or hold his son or daughter in my arms; I would never know the grandchildren that might have been. I would never see him impact the world as I know he could have. The past had been stolen, and the future would never be—and I was caught somewhere between the painful memories of yesterday and the broken dreams for the future.

## BROKEN DREAMS

Fantasizing about the future and daydreaming were some things that David and I did from time to time. We would allow our imaginations to run wild as we dreamed the biggest dreams we could imagine for the future. Sometimes our discussions were quite serious, while on other occasions we would laugh together as we considered ridiculous possibilities.

David was a very good student in school with a great deal of potential. I had high aspirations for him, and he could have achieved almost anything he set his mind to.

During one of our lighter times, I can remember saying, "David, I'll work real hard to take care of you while you're growing up. Then when you grow up, you become a doctor or some other highly successful professional. You earn lots of money and build a big house. Then I'll come and live with you. You can take care of me."

With a twinkle in his eye (always an indication that he was teasing) David responded, "You work real hard, Dad. I'll grow up and become a doctor or some other highly successful, highly paid professional. Then I'll make lots of money and build a big house for you and a big house for me!"

David loved life and had big dreams for his future. He looked forward to growing up and to the day when he would tower above me and call me "Shorty." But the possibility of that was cut off suddenly when David took his last breath and all his dreams came to an abrupt end.

## NOTHING'S QUITE THE SAME

Losing a child in death is one of the most traumatic and painful ordeals a parent can face in life. No matter how hard you try, life never returns to what you knew as "normal." I can tell you from personal experience that there is no way you could ever be prepared for such a loss.

When we think about death, we seldom, if ever, associate it with children. Dying is for old people, for those who have lived a long, full life, having realized and accomplished their dreams. How many times have you heard someone refer to the cause of death as "old age"? The loss of a child in death, however, is so unimaginable that no word even exists to convey that meaning. No word in the English language expresses that concept.

When a woman loses her husband, she is referred to as a widow; when a man loses his wife in death, he is called a widower. If both parents of a child die, that child is called an orphan. I know of no word in the English language that is synonymous with a parent who has lost a child. No word has ever been established to convey such indescribable loss.

For me, the sudden, senseless way in which David was stolen from our family only heightened my awareness of the profound pain that I faced day after day. At times I wondered if the pain and suffering would ever stop. Would it ever just go away and never return?

Most of the time I felt as if I were on the verge of tears, and it was not at all uncommon for me to suddenly burst into tears for no apparent reason. It was almost like suffering from a low-grade depression, and somehow the tears seemed to bring a temporary release. The best way I can explain it is in this way: if you feel as if you are about to sneeze, the longer you hold it, the more pain and discomfort there is. That's almost what the outbursts of tears did for me. They provided a way of ridding myself of some of my pent-up emotions and brought temporary relief. Then things would go better for a while. I'd have a good day and think, *I believe I'm getting better.* But inevitably, grief and the sense of loss were back at the door of my heart the next day, knocking loudly, making their presence known.

Life became a roller-coaster ride—an uncharted pathway of emotional highs and lows, with unexpected curves that played with my emotions. For me, some days were really up; then, without any warning, life would throw me a curve, and I would plunge to the depths of despair. This could be brought on by almost anything, and there was never a way to protect myself from the unexpected reminders that could overtake me at any time, any day, anywhere.

# PAINFUL MEMORIES

No one can really know what someone who has lost a loved one faces unless they have also faced a personal tragedy of similar magnitude. Losing someone whom you love more than your own life is painful beyond description. And when that loved one is gone, anything that was ever a part of his or her life can bring back memories to remind you of your loss: songs, places, expressions, colors, sports, favorite foods, a television program—the list is as endless as the experiences you have shared with the departed. Anything can trigger memories and grief, and often the things you take for granted can be the source of some of the most haunting reminders. Every time that happens, your healing process is interrupted. Let me share a few of the things I experienced along these lines.

Hearing a song can trigger those feelings of loss and hurt all over again. Although I love the song "Jesus, Lord to Me," each time I hear it I still can't help thinking about David. Why? Because that was the song the choir was singing as we walked down that long aisle on the day of the funeral.

Smelling a familiar fragrance or the aroma of certain foods can bring back vivid memories of that individual whom you have lost. Surfing the TV channels and seeing a sporting event or favorite team can remind you of good times you and your loved one shared in the past. It can also drive home the stark reality that your loved one is no longer there to share that activity with you.

No matter where you are, something potentially can serve as a reminder of your loss, regardless of whether or not your loved one was ever there with you. Once when I was in Seattle, I decided to go and see a movie because it seemed like a viable way to pass some time. The music from *St. Elmo's Fire* began playing, and I had to walk out of the theater. Although David and I had never physically been there in that theater together or in Seattle, the song was one of his favorites. Hearing it reminded me of him and how much I missed him.

One weekend while driving to Mt. Parrin to preach for Dr. Paul Walker, I turned on the car radio and heard an Atlanta Braves game broadcast. I immediately thought of David because he and I had spent so much time together watching the Atlanta Braves play. They were our favorite team, and we always followed their season closely together. Watching them play and cheering for them when they scored was something we often did. Happening upon that baseball game on the radio that day only brought the painful memories back.

Time after time something from everyday life would pop up as a glaring reminder that our lives would never return to what had once been considered normal. No matter what we did, something was always lurking around the next corner, ready to rip off the temporary mask that disguised reality and remind us that nothing would ever be the same.

## CARRYING ON

I finally realized that to go on, we would have to start rebuilding our lives with what we had left. That meant establishing a brand-new foundation for our lives as a family and starting some new traditions. Our past traditions had included David; some even centered on him. In no way did we want to forget David, but we just had to find a way to go on without him if we were going to survive. Nearly every part of life had to be readjusted in some way, and it was a constant challenge.

Through these times I learned to recognize some of the things that served as ongoing reminders of David's absence. As I identified them and began to talk about them, I gradually was able to deal with some of the painful reminders that kept interrupting my recovery.

Each day was a challenge, but as I grew stronger, I learned how to handle the painful memories. This strength helped me cope with things that had previously had a negative effect. It wasn't easy, but I was able to slowly but surely focus on the rebuilding process for my life, capturing one area at a time.

One such area was golf. As I mentioned in Chapter 1, the last day I saw David alive, Tony, David, and I played a game of golf together. This was an activity that we all enjoyed individually, so playing golf together was the epitome of fun. After David's death, however, I just couldn't go back. I had always enjoyed it, but I just couldn't make myself pick up a golf club and go back to the sport.

For months I stayed away from the golf course because the memories were just too painful to deal with. But I finally realized that Tony had enjoyed golf as much as David, and by ignoring the entire topic, I was causing Tony pain too. Consequently, after six months or more had passed since our final game with David, I invited Tony to play golf with me. I finally began to realize that I had been so consumed with my grief over David that I had neglected Tony in some ways. I had been almost oblivious to what he was going through, having lost his only brother. I knew I had to start thinking of him.

I'll never forget the look on his face when I mentioned golf. He looked surprised, but responded quickly with "Sure, Dad."

We grabbed our clubs and started to walk toward the car. As we did, I put my arm around Tony and said, "You know, Tony, I would have been just as heartbroken if it had been you in that car crash. There would have been no difference in how I felt. Now it's just you and me. David's gone, but we can make it if we stick together." And with that we took one giant step together toward a brighter tomorrow.

## "IF ONLY . . ."

That golf game represented just one victory in my war with sorrow and grief. I use the word *war* because war is typically understood to be a series of many battles and conflicts with an adversary that ultimately produces a victor.

Another foe I faced was the "if onlys," a struggle that King David also faced after his son died. Scripture provides this glimpse of King David's anguish. "Then the king was deeply moved, and went up to the chamber over the gate, and wept. And as he went, he said thus: "O my son Absalom—my son, my son Absalom—if only I had died in your place! O Absalom my son, my son!" (2 Samuel 18:33).

My struggle of "if onlys" was a difficult one, especially in the weeks and months immediately following David's death. It began almost as soon as I received that unforgettable telephone call, and I remember having similar feelings to those that King David expressed. "If only David hadn't gone out after church" . . . "If only I hadn't allowed him to drive until he was older" . . . "If only I'd been home that weekend" . . . "If only he would have come straight home from church instead of going out with his friends" . . . "If only the driver who killed him had been more responsible and had not driven while he was drunk" . . . "If only the drunk driver hadn't been going ninety miles an hour" . . . "If only there had been more light on the street that night" . . . "If only it had been me instead of David!"

But all the "if onlys" I considered didn't change the facts: David was gone, and life would never be the same again. Somehow I had to discover a way out of the dark tunnel that held me captive and find a way to go on.

## SEARCHING FOR ANSWERS

Recently while browsing through a book, I came upon some interesting facts that helped me understand myself better. I found that, according to the authors, the feelings and emotions I struggled with during that first year after David's death were fairly typical of most parents who have gone through the same life experiences.

Research conducted by Darrin R. Lehman of the University of California, Carmile B. Wortman of the University of Michigan, and others indicates that 62 percent of the parents they studied (all of whom had lost a child in an automobile accident) fell into this pattern. Four to seven years later, 28 percent of the parents were still running through the ways they could have saved their child.[1]

My "if only" questions led to another kind of question. I began to ask why. I wondered, "Why did God allow this? How could a tragedy like this happen to our family?" As a Christian and a minister of the gospel, I could not understand how God could allow this devastation to come upon our household. From the time I was a little boy, I made a choice to love and serve the Lord Jesus. To the best of my ability I had tried to do what was right. As I grew up, I had committed my life to full-time service, and I had been faithful to the work of the Lord, unlike some people I knew.

On one occasion I came in contact with a relative who also had a teenage son. I can recall thinking, *Why does he still have his son?* He had flirted with God and walked the line spiritually for years. I had done everything I could to stay in fellowship with the Lord and walk in His ways. Yet, why was I the one who lost a son?

## WHEN THE WHY BECOMES BIGGER THAN GOD

My questions of why continued, and no matter how I asked the question, there seemed to be no answer. "Why did God allow this?" . . . "Why does God allow tragedy?" . . . "Why did David die?" My questions went on and on.

For a time I think my focus was more on why than on God. In fact, as I look back now, I can see that I allowed the why to become bigger than God in a sense. My feeble attempt at second-guessing God didn't bring any answers to the surface. It still didn't answer the question, "Why David?"

As a preacher I knew that the Bible says, "There is an appointed time for everything. And there is a time for every event under heaven—A time to give birth, and a time to die; A time to plant, and a time to uproot what is planted" (Ecclesiastes 3:1–2 NASB). Yet, I didn't believe that God preset the time of David's death, for the Scriptures record, "It is appointed for men to die once, but after this the judgment" (Hebrews 9:27). God's Word says that death is certain, but Psalm 91:16 promises, "With long life I will satisfy him." Sixteen years certainly can't be viewed as long, so why had David's life been cut short and in such a tragic way?

## THE WRONG PLACE AT THE WRONG TIME

For nearly a year I asked God questions and searched for answers. Sometimes I thought about what I could have done to change the outcome. I tried to place the blame in several places, including the driver, who chose to operate his car while under the influence of alcohol. And at the end of that year of searching, I came to the only conclusion possible: David was in the wrong place at the wrong time.

I knew that life is made up of a series of choices and you can't control what other people do. Only that drunk driver had the decision-making ability to control what he did that night. When God gave man a free will, He endowed man with a capacity to originate choices and be responsible for his own actions.

Although that young man who chose to drive drunk that night was responsible for David's premature departure from life, David had also made a choice that was directly connected to passing from this life to eternity. The one question I never felt compelled to ask during that year of searching was "Where is David?" Why? Because I knew that he was "absent from the body and . . . present with the Lord" (2 Corinthians 5:8). David had always had a tender heart toward the Lord and had surrendered his life to Jesus Christ at an early age. Because of that decision, I knew that he was now a resident of an eternal city so magnificent that Scriptures say, "Eye has not seen, nor ear heard, / Nor have entered into the heart of man / The things which God has prepared for those who love Him" (1 Corinthians 2:9).

Having put aside all the questions and complex speculations

I had engaged in, I finally found solace in this resolve: David was just in the wrong place at the wrong time.

Once I had come to that resolve, the "if onlys" and the "whys" slowly vanished as each new day dawned. With the departure of these fading questions, I began to find strength to face each new day, and I finally began to look toward tomorrow with anticipation rather than dread.

## CHAPTER 4

# RISING ABOVE YOUR PROBLEMS

*I* never really understood what it was to suffer from depression—that is, until several months after David's death. It was at that point in my life that I discovered that depression is a problem that shows no respect for position or prominence, and it preys upon those who have been assailed by the problems and pressures of life. It is a uniquely human problem, one which man has faced throughout history.

When David was taken from us so suddenly, I experienced many different feelings and emotions that were totally foreign to me. Initially, I encountered shock. I was numb to everything around me. My shock soon turned into mourning, followed by sorrow and grief. Eventually, my grief over losing David turned into depression. Because I was a minister by vocation, I had spent many hours of my life counseling with those who had lost loved ones. In those situations I was able to bring a measure of comfort to the bereaved. But when I faced a personal loss, I didn't know what to do!

Recently, while paging through the book *Grieving, How to Go on Living when Someone You Love Dies*, I read the following information that helped me understand this period in my life when I faced severe depression. I was so depressed that I had no desire to go on with life. I have experienced this personally, I want to share it with you because I'm certain that it will be helpful to any reader who is facing similar feelings and circumstances.

> Acute grief typically includes painful yearning for your deceased loved one. You have excruciating loneliness for the person who died and for the unique relationship that has been lost. You have strong feelings of separation, deprivation, anguish, aching, and sadness. You are preoccupied with the deceased. You dream of him, think you have seen him, or actively search for him. Some people have overwhelming visual or auditory senses of their loved one. The pain is so bad that you feel nothing could help except the return of the deceased. Activities once pleasurable are no longer enjoyable. You may conclude that life is meaningless, and even that you, yourself, are worthless. You may become fearful that you will be overwhelmed by your mental suffering.[1]

That was me—Steve Brock! I was preoccupied with how much I missed David and was so depressed that, for years, almost anything could trigger my feelings of sorrow, causing me to lose control. In the twinkling of an eye, something could happen that would remind me of David, and instantly I would be in tears. I had a difficult time just coping with life, and I wondered what was wrong with me. I had never faced anything like this before in my life, and I didn't know if I was unique in experiencing these emotions. I feared that my life might always be that way, for I could see no way of escape.

But as I studied God's Word, I discovered that I was not alone. I found that many of the heroes of the Bible were not exempt from some of the same feelings I was experiencing. Elijah, for example, was a great prophet of God, filled with faith and power. He accomplished great feats of faith for God. He called down fire from heaven. He raised the widow's son from the dead. He was supernaturally fed by the ravens twice a day. All these and so many other great things happened through his life. Yet, when we study the Bible, we find that he was not always on the mountaintop of victory.

Scripture records a number of instances where God supernaturally intervened on behalf of Elijah. God used him mightily, and he was an anointed man of God. But when he faced a personal crisis, his boldness vanished, and he hid from his problems.

At one point in my life, I tried to hide from my pain and problems too. I became miserable and depressed, and wondered if God could ever use me again. I questioned whether or not I could go on, just as Elijah did.

It was at that moment that I realized if God could rescue Elijah and use him in such a mighty way, even though he had almost given up at one point, He could also rescue me and use me to bring a message of hope to those in despair.

## ELIJAH, GOD'S MESSENGER OF HOPE

The account of Elijah's life found in 1 Kings includes dynamic stories of victory and supernatural provision. Let's take a moment and look at the highlights in 1 Kings 17.

When Elijah hid by the Brook Cherith, God sent ravens to feed him. Twice a day the ravens brought bread and meat to him.

When drought caused the brook to dry up, God chose to provide for Elijah through the widow of Zarephath. God provided for him and sustained the widow and her son with the barrel of meal and cruse of oil that never ran out until the day that the Lord sent rain upon the earth, ending the drought.

Some time later, God used Elijah to restore life to the widow's son who had become sick and died. As Elijah called upon God, life came back into the boy's body—a miracle took place! The boy was restored to his mother miraculously!

## THE ULTIMATE CHALLENGE

One of the stories I most enjoy studying about Elijah was the day he had a showdown with the prophets of Baal. Because the children of Israel had begun to forsake the commandments of the Lord and follow Baal, Elijah told Ahab to send all of Israel and the prophets of Baal to Mount Carmel. He boldly challenged the 450 prophets of Baal to a contest to determine, before all who would gather on Mount Carmel, who the real God was.

Ahab accepted and the challenge began. Elijah watched as the prophets of Baal prepared for the contest. He looked on as 450 men stood around an altar of sacrifice, cutting themselves, begging Baal to send down fire upon their sacrifices and prove that he was God.

Hour after hour nothing happened. In desperation the false prophets of Baal cried out all the louder and continued to beg and plead with Baal. But regardless of what the prophets of Baal did, no fire fell to consume their sacrifice. They cried louder and cut themselves, mutilating their bodies, but nothing happened.

While all this commotion was going on with the prophets of Baal, Elijah mocked them, saying "Perhaps *your* god has gone on a journey, or perhaps he's asleep. Speak a little louder, and he might wake up!" Elijah was bold, and his faith in God kept him strong.

When it was Elijah's turn, he called all the people together. He invited them to watch as he ordered a deep trench to be dug around the sacrifice. When it was finished, he commanded that the sacrifice and the altar be drenched with water—not once, not twice, but three times. Then he called upon the God of Abraham, Isaac, and Israel, saying "Let it be known this day that You are God in Israel and I am Your servant, and that I have done all these things at Your word" (1 Kings 18:36).

Scripture records, "Then the fire of the LORD fell and consumed the burnt sacrifice, and the wood and the stones and the dust, and it licked up the water that was in the trench. Now when all the people saw it, they fell on their faces; and they said, 'The LORD, He is God! The LORD, He is God!'" (1 Kings 18:38–39).

Elijah saw miracle after miracle take place during the course of his ministry. He may have been somewhat unorthodox, but he was bold, and he had faith in God for the impossible. And the impossible took place, as long as his faith was established in God. But when he wavered, he took a sudden detour to potential destruction.

## DETOUR TO DESPAIR

In the nineteenth chapter of 1 Kings we find a very different picture of Elijah. The bold prophet of God whom we found in 1 Kings 18 suddenly became a man who was praying to die! After the greatest victory of his life, this prophet of God "went a day's journey into the wilderness, and came and sat down under a broom tree. And he prayed that he might die, and said, 'It is enough! Now, LORD, take my life, for I am no better than my fathers!'" (1 Kings 19:4).

Elijah was so depressed and confused that he just wanted to die. As I said before, depression is a problem that shows no respect for position or prominence, and it preys upon those who have been assailed by the problems and pressures of life. One prevailing question in today's emotionally shell-shocked age is: "I don't know why I feel so depressed. Is there anything I can do about it?"

Yes, there is. You can remind yourself that everyone experiences depression at various times to some degree, even great men of God like the prophet Elijah.

There is a tendency to picture Bible characters as super humans, as though they were from another planet—especially a man like Elijah. After all, didn't God send ravens to feed him? Didn't God use him to raise a widow's son from the dead? Wasn't he the one who withstood the 450 prophets of Baal, praying down fire from heaven one day and rain the next? Yet he was in such despair and depression that he wanted to die!

At times, even a man of unusual faith like Elijah can be subject to depression. Plainspoken James put Elijah in the proper perspective when he reminded his readers that Elijah "was a man subject to like passions as we are" (James 5:17 KJV). The

Contemporary English Version says: "Elijah was just as human as we are."

The irrationality of Elijah's wish to die is reflected in the remaining verses of that chapter. Had he really wanted God to take his life, he needed only to have run a little more slowly as he was fleeing for his life, and Jezebel gladly would have had him beheaded.

Elijah didn't really want to die. I think he was simply experiencing neurotic depression. In his case it didn't last very long, for only a few days later he would reflect a much more optimistic mood and ministry. All he needed was a little rest, some food, and supernatural ministry. Suddenly life was worth living, and he was able to hear God's voice again.

## DO CHRISTIANS GET DEPRESSED?

I know what it's like to experience depression, to feel as if you are drowning in a sea of despair with nothing to live for. Each individual may not encounter depression to the same degree or in the same way that I did, but I believe that no matter what label is attached to these kinds of feelings, everyone at some time experiences some level of depression.

I once heard that approximately one-fifth of the American population is crippled periodically or temporarily by depression. Depression, even when it is temporary, can include changes in an individual such as a lower activity level, feelings of sadness, dejection, or varying degrees of worthlessness. Some individuals may find they are laughing one minute and on the verge of tears the next. This is typical of someone who is experiencing temporary depression. Because of how you perceive your situation during these times, you may feel that there is no end in sight to your troubles. In helpless desperation you give in to the tears that accompany feelings of such hopelessness.

The tragic results of this tormenting crippler are told by the fact that our national suicide rate ranks among the highest in the world. This not only emphasizes our need to detect the early symptoms of depression but should also encourage us to deal with them effectively, in both the natural and supernatural realms.

## Physical Causes

I'm told that some depression has its roots in physical sources. Abraham Lincoln's observation was a good one: "A weary body makes for a weary mind." Physical and mental fatigue can leave a person feeling depressed. This may have been part of Elijah's problem.

A significant amount of attention has recently been given to studying body rhythms. There is increasing evidence that each person's life proceeds through a unique cycle of high and low moods, influenced at times by physical factors like body fluid levels as well as psychological factors.

In examining your own body rhythm, remember that mood cycles seldom extend longer than four days. Depression limited to such a brief period may well be attributed to body rhythms.

## Emotional Causes

Although fear and guilt are frequently part of depression, some doctors say that the predominant emotional reason for depression is often anger. Individuals whose depression is largely psychological in origin are basically very angry people.

In some cases, the same might be said about people who are not depressed. They, too, sometimes have just as much anger to deal with. The basic difference between the two groups lies in what they do with their anger and how they handle it. The people who are not depressed have discovered constructive ways of directing their angry feelings, while depressed people frequently express their anger inwardly.

## Spiritual Causes

Another contributor to depression can be found in the spiritual dimension of a person's life. Any physical or psychological weakness a person may be experiencing is often seized upon by satanic forces to lure the already discouraged person into thoughts of condemnation. John described Satan's tactics accurately when he said that Satan was "the accuser of our brethren" (Revelation 12:10). Job encountered Satan this way on more than one occasion, and so did Elijah.

## COPING WITH DEPRESSION

How can a person cope with depression? At times you may feel as if you are the only one who ever gets discouraged and depressed. You must know this simply is not true.

We all face varying degrees of depression occasionally, and there are some things you and I can do to overcome this divisive foe when it knocks at our door.

*Trust God's love.* You can't earn it, but no one is excluded from it.

*Season your life with prayer.* "The effective, fervent prayer of a righteous man [or woman] avails much" (James 5:16).

*Don't condemn yourself.* You're not sinful because you are depressed.

*Don't try to figure things out.* You'll never solve the mysteries of life and the universe. Praise God anyhow!

*Plunge into physical activity.* Much of a person's depression stems from his angry feelings. Anger is an energy producer. When this energy is spent scrubbing and waxing the floor, mowing the lawn, washing the car, playing tennis or golf, swimming, or in similar high-energy activities, it will produce more constructive results.

*Make yourself available to others.* When you help others, you help yourself.

*Monitor what you think about.* "Finally, brethren, whatever things are true, whatever things are noble, whatever things are just, whatever things are pure, whatever things are lovely, whatever things are of good report, if there is any virtue and if there is anything praiseworthy—*meditate on these things*" (Philippians 4:8, italics mine).

*Avoid "pity parties."* Self-pity can be destructive. Don't isolate yourself; get involved with people. This is one area in which I allowed myself to be extremely vulnerable.

Being alone leads to self-pity. Elijah found the going tough when he was alone under the broom tree, and he became depressed. In my case, loneliness became a stepping-stone to self-pity. This, in turn, became the catalyst to depression, leading to a very difficult time in my life. Let me explain.

It was when self-pity was in full bloom that I had my greatest battle with anger. I was angry with God, angry with life, angry with myself, angry that David was gone, angry that I was still alive, and much more. No matter how badly I felt, regardless of how much I indulged in self-pity, I couldn't do anything about the circumstances in my life, and that only added to my anger.

I did everything I could to control and suppress my anger. Sometimes I felt only sputtering irritation, but at other times I was so angry I felt white-hot rage, often for no apparent reason. But no matter what level of anger I felt, I tried to suppress it as best I could. Little did I know that suppressing my anger was one of the worst things I could do. My suppressed anger became a strong force and eventually led to depression.

Rather than suppress my anger, I should have talked about it. Internalizing it did absolutely no good for anyone. Having gone through this, I encourage any reader who may be battling with suppressed anger and depression to do two things:

1. Admit when you are depressed.
2. Talk about it. As you open up and talk about this destructive force, you will undoubtedly discover the source of your depression. Perhaps the solution is as simple as going to a place that was a favorite of your deceased loved one or one that you often visited together. Figure out how to deal with your feelings in that place, and learn how to handle it.

Remember the incident I shared in Chapter 3 regarding how difficult it was to resume the game of golf? Although it took nearly six months for me to return to the game and to that golf course where David and I spent our last day on earth together, I finally found a way to handle it. When I did, it did as much good for me as it did for Tony: it brought a measure of healing to both of us.

*Lean on God and His church.* The believer's prescription for recovery from depression closely follows the pattern of Elijah's experience. The most lasting relief is to be found by rediscovering that both God and man can be trusted to love us and help provide for our needs.

## DEPRESSION IN TODAY'S WORLD

The pressures of modern living and the social upheavals of our generation are producing an increasing incidence of depression-related problems. Occasionally, there are medical reasons for depression, but often it is a darkness of the soul and of the mind, affecting men and women of all ages—Christians and non-Christians alike.

Depression is no new problem, for even in Bible times men like David, Paul, Elijah, Job, and Peter all suffered from it at one time or another. For example, Paul had established the church at Corinth and was traveling to Troas to meet Titus so they could continue to spread the gospel. But when he arrived, Titus wasn't there (2 Corinthians 2:12–13).

Paul continued on to Macedonia, assuming that Titus would be there. But when he arrived, Titus wasn't there either. This apparently troubled Paul greatly, for in this portion of Scripture he makes reference to his feelings on the matter.

The Phillips translation says: "For even when we arrived in Macedonia, we found no rest but trouble all around us—wrangling outside and anxiety within. Nevertheless God, who cheers the depressed, gave us the comfort of the arrival of Titus" (2 Corinthians 7:5–6). The New King James Version says, "Nevertheless God, who comforts the downcast, comforted us by the coming of Titus."

Paul literally gives the symptoms of depression in this verse, but he also proves that victory over depression is possible when the matter is surrendered to God and He takes control.

## TYPES OF DEPRESSION

There are varying opinions on the topic of depression and what contributes to it. Therefore, I want to focus only on three kinds of depression and discuss each one briefly.

### Emotional Depression

The first type is emotional depression, which I feel is produced primarily by loneliness. It can sometimes be brought on by disappointment, either in ourselves or someone else. For example, in Scripture we find that the man at the pool of Bethesda spoke out of loneliness when he said, "I have no man to put me into the pool" (John 5:7).

We can find another example in the life of Elijah. He knew the dark clouds of emotional depression even after the miracle on Mount Carmel when he complained to God and said, "I, even I only, am left" (1 Kings 19:10b KJV).

In emotional depression David said, "Thou hast put away mine acquaintance far from me" (Psalm 88:8 KJV). Job made the same statement in Job 19:13 when referring to the trials he faced.

Each of these men felt alone and mistakenly believed that no one cared about them. I have experienced these same kinds of emotions, and I assure you that it is very deceptive and difficult to identify.

## Mental Depression

Mental depression is the second kind of depression I want to discuss. It sometimes can grip our understanding and bring confusion. We begin to ask, "Why did God allow this? Why am I suffering so?" We become consumed with our questions, and before long, the why becomes bigger than God in our lives.

I struggled with this for some time, as I shared in Chapter 3. I was looking for someone to blame for much of what I experienced as a result of David's death. Because my emotional makeup was so complex at that time, I sought a complex answer to my questions. I attempted to second-guess the circumstances, considered a number of "if only" propositions, and even tried to bear some of the blame myself for not protecting my son from harm. I didn't actually find any relief from that mental depression until I finally came to the realization that my son David was just in the wrong place at the wrong time.

## Spiritual Depression

Perhaps the most difficult type of depression for a Christian to overcome is spiritual depression. When a believer experiences spiritual depression, it seems that God is no longer real to him; he has become accustomed to the presence of God and only goes through the motions of a mechanical Christian experience.

Spiritual depression can be caused by a number of things including not being right with God, unseen barriers, a lack of dedication, believing the lies of the enemy, a failure of commitment, or having something against our brother or sister in the Lord.

It is not God's will that any man should be bowed down with the load of dark depression. God never intended for the Christian to be imprisoned by anything, but to be totally free. The Bible says "If the Son makes you free, you shall be free indeed" (John 8:36). This freedom is without reservation.

## THE ENEMY'S BATTLE PLAN

The enemy's arena of war is no ordinary battlefield. It is in your mind, and his weapons consist of lies and deceptions. The battlefield of your mind is where Satan is constantly at work, repeatedly firing thoughts that harass, disturb, and tear down. If the devil can bring a dark cloud of depression between a believer and the Lord, then his attack on the mind has succeeded.

There are no words that wound more deeply than those that suggest that God has forsaken us. The enemy knows that if he can make us doubt God's loving care, he will have scored a victory over us. He would have us believe that every evil force has joined hands with him to stand against us.

At times we are like the disciples who, in the midst of a tumultuous storm, said to Jesus: "Do You not care that we are perishing?" (Mark 4:38). Peter was on board during that storm and undoubtedly questioned Jesus' concern for him and the others. Yet he later wrote, "Cast all your anxiety on him because he cares for you" (1 Peter 5:7 NIV).

Notice this thought: such a question is very often the echo of something the enemy has said. He may not have said it to us directly. He simply got someone to say in our hearing, "His God is no help to him now."

Had Satan come to us directly and said, "There is no help for you in God," we probably would have withstood him to his face. But he uses this sly method to discourage us. Often people lose hope because they listen to what others say.

There is a solution to this dilemma. We must take our eyes off the enemy and his host and fix them on the Lord.

The Bible declares, "You will keep him in perfect peace, whose mind is stayed on You" (Isaiah 26:3). *The Living Bible* says, "He will keep in perfect peace all those who trust in him, whose thoughts turn often to the Lord!"

## THE ULTIMATE ANSWER

There is an answer to depression: it's faith in Jesus Christ. King David, who faced many great crises in life, some of his own making and others outside of his influence, said, "I would have lost heart, unless I had believed / That I would see the goodness of the LORD / In the land of the living" (Psalm 27:13). David fought against depression with faith.

Depression can also be conquered through fellowship. Don't lock yourself up in a dungeon of depression; enjoy the fellowship of God's people. One of the classic symptoms of chronic depression is that a person seeks to shut himself away from others, avoiding contact with friends and even relatives.

Depression is conquered by learning how to relate our lives to Christ. We are the children of God; we are sons and daughters of the King of glory; we are joint heirs with Christ; we are flesh of His flesh; bone of His bone; God is our Father; Jesus Christ is our Elder Brother; the Holy Spirit is our Comforter. What more do we need?

Let's look at the example of Elijah for a moment. When Elijah faced despair and depression, God revealed Himself to Elijah in three ways (1 Kings 19:4–18):

1. *God provided for his needs.* He made sure that Elijah had food, water, and shelter. Elijah did not have to worry about how to sustain his life.
2. *God spoke to Elijah in a still small voice.* At times we want God to speak to us with the intensity of a roaring cannon, when it is the inner witness of the Holy Spirit that bears assurance of faith. Romans 8:16 states "The Spirit Himself bears witness with our spirit that we are children of God."

**3.** *God showed Elijah that he wasn't alone.* Although he initially believed that he stood alone against the prophets of Baal, he eventually discovered seven thousand prophets in Israel who hadn't bowed to Baal.

## THE PROMISE

You and I are never alone either. In Matthew 28:20 we find these marvelous words of assurance from Christ: "Lo, I am with you always, even to the end of the age." These words are our insurance policy against loneliness. "I am with you *always*"— forever. You can't get a better commitment than that from anyone!

No matter what situations or pain you may face in life, don't allow the enemy to tell you that you are all alone. Remember, Jesus promised to be with you and me forever. That means He will be with us every day here on earth, as well as throughout eternity.

## THE LIGHT OF HIS LOVE

Jesus said, "I am the light of the world. He who follows Me shall not walk in darkness, but have the light of life" (John 8:12).

That "light of life" was available to me, and it is available to you as well. Jesus was ready to turn the spotlight of His love on my life and destroy the darkness of depression that loomed over me. His gentle, perfect love was ready to transform my disposition, my direction, and my destiny.

But that was not possible until I came to the end of myself and reached a turning point—and that didn't happen until New Year's Day.

## CHAPTER 5

# DON'T WRITE MY EPITAPH JUST YET!

*C*hristmas 1986 was a time of survival for the Brock family. Because it was our first Christmas without David, it was a very difficult time for all of us. It had been only five months since David's death, and the sense of loss was heightened by the holidays, which had always been a special time in our home. The holidays are said to be some of the most difficult times for those who have lost a loved one. I know from experience that this is absolute fact.

As a family we had always looked forward to Christmas and this time of year. Christmas Eve was our special time to celebrate Christmas as a family. Everything we did in preparation for the holidays, including the shopping, went into making Christmas special. But shopping and decorating were unthinkable for us that year. Christmas was supposed to be a joyful time, a time of festivities, laughter, and celebration. But without David, what did we have to be happy about?

## COUNTDOWN TO CHRISTMAS

As Christmas got closer and closer, we ignored the whole topic of celebrating and shopping. From time to time, someone would mention that there were only a certain number of shopping days left, giving the number. But it didn't matter to any of us how close Christmas was. We were doing our best to avoid any memory of how Christmas used to be. Our goal was purely to survive.

Pat and I waited until the last minute before we finally attempted to do something constructive regarding Christmas. We felt that we had to make some effort for Tony's sake. He had experienced the same loss but had suffered in ways different from those that Pat and I faced. Although we missed David terribly, especially at this time of year, at least Pat and I had each other. This year Tony would be the only child, a role that was foreign to him.

For fifteen years he and David had enjoyed Christmas together. When they were little, they giggled together next to the Christmas tree as they experimented with their new toys. Later as teenagers, they teased each other as they distributed the gifts and helped one another get their newest electronic acquisition running just as soon as the wrapping paper had been removed. But this year, everything was different.

Finally on Christmas Eve we pulled ourselves together enough in the late afternoon to get in the car and drive to a local store that was still open. We wanted to buy some gifts for Tony and his girlfriend, Gwen (who is now his wife). She had graciously offered to spend Christmas with us. (As I reflect on that time now, I think she decided to spend Christmas with us so we would have four individuals as we had always had, rather than the three we were being forced to grow accustomed to.)

As the store was about to close on Christmas Eve, we hurried through the aisles and bought a few gifts. Then we returned home to make our final preparations for the holidays.

## CHRISTMAS AND THE WEEKEND AFTER

We managed to get through Christmas Eve and Christmas Day, surviving every aspect of the holiday festivities. Our Christmas dinner on Christmas Eve included polite conversation by each of us as we dined on turkey and all the trimmings. The table talk was a bit strained, but no one acknowledged that. We were each trying to make the day as normal as possible, although *normal* was a word that no longer had any real significance to any of us.

After dinner we retired to the family room to share our Christmas gifts with one another. Tony and Gwen distributed the gifts, and we carefully opened each package. Tony and Gwen's presence helped Pat and me a great deal and, as I recall, we even laughed a little from time to time.

But even though we were able to muster a laugh or two, Christmas at our house was much different this year because David wasn't there. But if survival was the goal (and for me it was), it was a mission accomplished. We managed to survive the Christmas dinner, the gifts, and everything else that was a part of the holiday celebration. Eventually we unplugged the Christmas tree, turned out the lights, and said farewell to Christmas 1986!

The day *after* Christmas was a different story, however. David's absence from our home and this special family holiday overwhelmed me almost like billowing waves swallowing a boat on a storm-tossed sea. I fell apart. I felt so empty inside, so alone—and how I missed David!

I had experienced many bad days since David's death, days filled with grief and pain. But what I was feeling now seemed much worse and more complex. My heart ached for him because I missed him so. Yet, at the same time, I felt angry because he had been stolen from us and we couldn't enjoy this special time of year with him. In addition, I was depressed and disappointed that I couldn't pull myself together enough to deal with the emotions connected to everything I was feeling. I felt as if I were on the verge of tears all the time, and at times I began crying for no apparent reason. I couldn't bring myself to talk to Pat about anything. She didn't seem to have her usual Christmas cheer and excitement, so I knew that she must be having her own struggles. I stayed to myself because I knew I wasn't much fun to be around. Besides, I didn't have much to say about anything, so I just internalized my feelings and tried to hide my fragile, fragmented emotions, masking them as best I could.

I did my best to stay focused and busy. I tried to keep my mind on other things—anything but David. But that failed miserably because Christmas vacation had always been a time that the boys and I shared. The obvious lack of vacation activities only reminded me that David wasn't there.

As a last resort, I focused on my itinerary for the upcoming weeks, which included a New Year's Eve service that I had scheduled several months before. I was to be the special guest at a church in Washington State on New Year's Eve. My part in the evening included the preaching and singing, so I put all my energy into getting ready for that service.

As I reviewed my calendar, I also discovered that I had made a commitment for a guest appearance on TBN's *Praise the Lord* program on December 30. Consequently, I had to leave home a day early and go through Dallas for the television program before going on to Washington for the weekend.

*Praise the Lord* is a daily program on the Trinity Broadcasting Network (TBN) that features a variety of hosts from across America. That evening Dan and Bonnie Schaefer of Oklahoma City were hosting the program. They pastor a thriving church in Oklahoma City, which they also founded. I had known them for a number of years, and Pat and I have always regarded them as wonderful friends.

As our friends, they were aware of the tragedy our family had faced in July when David was taken from us. From time to time during the interview portion of the program, they made an occasional reference to David and to our family. At one point I remember them asking, "With everything that has happened this year, how did you and your family make it through this Christmas season?"

Their other comments about losing David hadn't really called for a response from me. The question, however, caught me off guard, and I wasn't sure how to handle it. I was hurting inside, but I just couldn't bring myself to talk about it, especially on national television. So to avoid the topic, I told them that we were doing great and our holidays had gone quite well, considering everything. I was determined to get through the program as best I could and avoid talking about the pain that was gnawing at me.

I sang a song or two, we talked about something or other, and the program finally came to an end. I was relieved! I had survived the evening and the questions. Now all I had to do was make it through New Year's Eve! So with the television program behind me, I was off to Washington.

## ON TO WASHINGTON

I flew to Seattle the next day to fulfill my weekend commitment. I don't remember much about the flight except that I cried all the way from Dallas to Seattle.

I was lost in my own world, unaware of everything around me on the airplane. I was only conscious of the pain that I felt deep inside; it seemed to increase with each passing minute. By the time the plane landed in Seattle and I got off, I was in total agony. In fact, I was hurting so badly that I remember literally shaking my fist in the face of God that day as I said, "God, You don't love me. You let David die!" In my head and from past experience I knew that the Lord promises to be our strength and will help us in our time of need, but this time my heart hurt so badly, I didn't even ask for help. I just wanted to be left alone to suffer all by myself.

But the enemy of my soul had another idea. At the time I didn't realize that the pain of losing David wasn't the real source of my torment, although his death had been the most painful experience of my life. I was about to discover that beyond the endless pain lurked the real enemy in the shadows, waiting to pounce on me when I was at my weakest point. This enemy can always be found prowling in the shadowy recesses of life. He had attacked me on many previous occasions, but this time I didn't recognize his tactics. I was hurting too much.

Because the New Year's Eve service at the church was to be the highlight of the weekend there in Washington, I tried to stay very focused as I got ready for the service. I made it through the evening, and the people who attended seemed to enjoy the service, including the pastor.

Following the service, I returned to my hotel room, physically exhausted from the travel and my busy weekend. I collapsed into bed and slept away the few hours that remained of the night. I was exhausted, emotionally and physically, and my slumber provided a temporary place of solace from my pain.

## JANUARY 1, 1987

Holidays are a terrible time to be away from home, and New Year's Day is one of the worst! By this time I had discovered that I could cope with one day at a time as long as I stayed busy. But as you probably know, there's almost nothing to do on New Year's Day! I was restless because I didn't know what to do. I didn't want to watch the televised games either, because every year until this year, I had always tried to watch the football games with my boys.

In desperation I finally phoned a friend named Nancy Harmon who lived in the Portland, Oregon, area. Nancy is a singer, and she and her singing group lived there. We had sung together on many occasions and enjoyed some great times together.

I was thrilled when she answered the telephone. After a brief conversation she told me her singing group was getting together for dinner and invited me to join them. I couldn't stand the thought of being alone, so I gladly accepted the invitation.

I got into my rental car and drove to Portland from my Seattle hotel. They graciously waited for me to arrive before eating, so we ate almost as soon as I arrived. When we had finished eating, some of the guys from her group hurried away from the table to watch the New Year's Day games while the women tidied up the kitchen. Although I wasn't particularly eager to watch the football games, I didn't want to be rude, so I joined them and tried to forget about my aching, empty heart that missed David.

Unfortunately, it didn't work. New Year's Day and the football games were almost synonymous with David's memory. We had always watched every football game possible together, and today things just didn't seem right without David.

I sat there as game after game came on. From time to time the guys around me would cheer for a touchdown, an interception, or some incredible play by one of the teams. The teams were playing great football from all indications, but I just didn't feel that I was a part of what was happening around me. After doing everything I could to fill the day and my thoughts, in the hope that something would help me forget my pain and loss, I finally thanked Nancy and her group for a nice day and excused myself.

I got back into my rental car and started for the hotel in Seattle. It had been a long day, and I was emotionally spent. I finally arrived at my hotel and went straight to my room. It was late, and I hoped that sleep would help mask the pain and grief that I had dealt with all day.

I locked the door to the hotel room and prepared to retire for the night. Before climbing into bed, I sat down on the side of the bed for just a moment—a moment that I will never forget. Something swept over me with such intensity as my emotions gave way to my inner pain. *I can't make it,* I thought. *I just can't make it!*

I don't know how long I sat there—seconds perhaps, or maybe several minutes. I can't say for sure, but as I sat there a violent conflict raged upon the battlefield of my mind.

A destructive voice whispered, "You can't go on. Give up. Life's not worth living anymore!"

*No, that's not right,* I thought.

"But what have you got to live for? You know you can't make it!" the enemy of my soul said accusingly.

*But I have to go on,* I argued.

"Why? You're just a loser. Come on—give up!"

## A FIGHT TO THE FINISH

At another time or in another place I might have been stronger and more equipped to fight. But in that hotel room so far from home, I felt utterly alone and vulnerable. It didn't really seem to matter that I was a minister of the gospel who knew that God's Word contained promises like:

> *God is our refuge and strength,*
> *A very present help in trouble.* (Psalm 46:1)

> *The LORD is my light and my salvation;*
> *Whom shall I fear?*
> *The LORD is the strength of my life;*
> *Of whom shall I be afraid?* (Psalm 27:1)

That night, all alone in Seattle at that time of year, I felt so alone and so insecure. I really didn't know if I could go on. Rather than boldly declaring, "I can do all things through Christ who strengthens me" (Philippians 4:13), I felt more like the psalmist David when he said:

> *O LORD, God of my salvation,*
> *I have cried out day and night before You.*
> *Let my prayer come before You;*
> *Incline Your ear to my cry.*
> *For my soul is full of troubles,*
> *And my life draws near to the grave.*
> *I am counted with those who go down to the pit;*
> *I am like a man who has no strength.* (Psalm 88:1–5)

I don't know how much time passed, but I remember that I finally stood up and got dressed. As I thought about all my options, I decided I just couldn't go on. In that hotel room at that moment, I didn't think I could face another day. I just couldn't make it, and suicide seemed like the only answer left for me!

Consumed with self-pity and eaten up by loneliness, I decided to get some pills. I decided that I was willing to go wherever I had to go to find them at that time of the night. Then I'd come back to my room and take as many as necessary to end all the pain and grief.

I put on my jacket and reached for the car keys. Then, as I headed for the door of that hotel room, a fleeting thought passed through my mind: *What about Tony and Pat at home? What will this do to them?*

Although I was thinking primarily of myself at that moment, I didn't want to hurt them. I wanted a way out of all the pain, grief, and loneliness so badly, but how could I do something like this to those whom I loved most?

## ONE MORE CHANCE

*I guess I ought to try God one more time,* I thought as the door started to close slowly behind me. I turned around and reached for the doorknob. Stepping back inside my room, I closed the door and put down the car keys.

As I walked over and sat down on the side of the bed again, these words came to mind: *call Paul and Jan.* I regarded Paul and Jan Crouch as dear friends. But as the founders of Trinity Broadcasting Network (TBN), one of the foremost Christian broadcasting networks, I knew that they were always traveling. They had given me their home telephone number a month before, but their busy schedule didn't allow them much time at home.

*Call Paul and Jan.* The words kept echoing in my mind. I didn't even know if I still had the number, but I finally reached for my briefcase. I opened it and sorted through some miscellaneous notes and papers inside. As I continued to look for the number, I reasoned that because they traveled all the time, they were most likely away at this time of year. But if I could find their number, I'd make the call.

Midway through the stack of papers and notes, I found the telephone number they had jotted down for me. I closed the briefcase and moved toward the telephone. Then I slowly dialed the number and waited, counting each time the phone rang. *Ring ... ring ... ring ... ring ... ring ...* and after it rang the fifth time, I heard someone answer.

"Hello?" answered the familiar voice on the other end of the line. It was Jan Crouch!

"Oh, hello, Jan," I said, surprised to hear her voice. "I didn't know if you would be home today."

Jan responded with her usual warmth, telling me that they were normally not home. After another statement or two, the tone of her voice changed rather suddenly, and she asked, "How are you doing, Steve?" There was an obvious note of concern in her voice.

"OK ... ," I said hesitantly.

"Just OK?" Jan asked. As her voice trailed off, I hesitated for a moment and then began to weep.

Through my tears I heard warm, loving words that cut through all my heartache. The familiar voice was Jan's, but I knew deep within my heart that the words being spoken were straight from the throne room of heaven—they were words from the heart of God.

"My grace is sufficient for you. You can make it! I need you to tell other people My grace is sufficient and that they can make it." As Jan spoke, I felt as if God Himself was speaking through her. Each word gripped me deeply, bringing such life and unexplainable hope. She paused for a moment, and then began to speak authoritatively. "Steve, the Lord shows me that you are sitting on the side of a bed in a hotel room. There is a big evil presence lurking over you that wants to take your life. But when the Holy Spirit spoke through me just now, that evil presence left, and you are free!"

And I was! Instantaneously I began to laugh. I laughed and laughed for fifteen minutes as the gloom and pain left and a freedom that I had not known since July 27 flooded through me. In a moment, the heavy burdens of sorrow that I had carried rolled away, and I suddenly felt as if a fountain of joy was bubbling up from deep within. My sadness was gone, and I had a reason to go on. I had a reason to live!

The next day I awoke with a different outlook on life. I got into my rental car and drove to the airport to catch my plane home. As I drove along, I thanked my heavenly Father for His faithfulness and care for me. I felt freer than I had felt in months. I didn't feel empty any longer, and the pain of losing David wasn't as severe as it had been.

Alone in the car, talking to the Lord and praying, I sensed Him whispering these words to me: "The best way to remember David is to look forward to seeing him again, for you will one day. Stop wallowing in your self-pity. Stay close to Me or that same evil presence will try to take your life again."

As I got on the airplane and headed for home, I felt different. The sad emptiness was gone. I didn't sit there and cry uncontrollably as I had done when I flew to Seattle just days earlier. Oh, yes, I still missed David, but today that sense of loss didn't consume me as it had in the past. As the plane reached cruising altitude, I sat there, thinking about my wonderful wife, Pat, and my son Tony, at home. I'd be home in just a few hours, and I couldn't wait to see them. I was glad that we would be together, the three of us.

As the plane continued to make its way toward home, I rehearsed in my mind what it would be like today when I got off the plane. Pat and Tony would be there waiting for me, and the thought of seeing them again made me happy. As I mused about seeing them again, my mind drifted to a day in the future when there would be an even greater reunion—a day when Pat, Tony, I, and David would be reunited—a day when the four of us would once again stand together. But this time it wouldn't be in our home in Ohio. It would be in our eternal home—heaven. This time we would be standing around the throne of God, and we would be reunited *forever*!

## GATE 4 AGAIN

When the plane landed in Cincinnati, I gathered my things and left the airplane. I walked up the ramp and into the airport, down the long, familiar concourse past Gate 4 as I had done so many times before.

As I walked past Gate 4, my mind flashed back to five months earlier when Tony and I had taken this same walk. That day the concourse had seemed to go on forever, and we had dreaded what awaited us at the other end. But this time it was different. I had a spring in my step, I held my head high, and I walked differently. I had a sense of purpose, and I felt as if I had begun living an entirely new life. I knew beyond a shadow of a doubt that God truly loved me, that He cared for me, and above all, I knew I could make it! And if I could make it, that meant Pat, Tony, and I could make it together!

The pain that had come to be such a familiar part of each day had finally begun to ease, and for that I was so grateful. This was the day I had waited for so long—the day my miracle began.

Only hours before I had felt like a loser, hopeless and ready to give up. But now I knew that with God's help, I was a winner and I could make it.

As I walked toward the baggage claim area, I thought, *Satan, you tried to finish me off. You tried to write my epitaph as a permanent loser, but the battle's over and you've lost! You're defeated, and I'm the winner!*

## CHAPTER 6

# WHERE ARE ALL MY FRIENDS?

*I* *haven't heard from my friend. I wonder why he hasn't phoned when I'm hurting so? He must have heard about David . . .*

These words echoed the cry of my heart in the days immediately following David's death. So many people from many different places had taken the time to call or contact Pat and me to express their sympathy after David's death. Some callers were acquaintances while others were people whom I had never met. They were just concerned viewers of Trinity Broadcasting Network (TBN) who had seen "Pray for the Brocks" at the bottom of their television screen on July 28, 1986, the day after we lost David. TBN had run a continuous crawler on the screen throughout the day, so the news of our tragedy spread very quickly. And whether Pat and I knew them or not, their words of love and kindness helped to bring comfort to our aching hearts.

Even though so many called or contacted us, a number of our friends I was certain would call never did. This was most surprising to me, and in the midst of my grief I found myself asking, "Where are all my friends? Why haven't they called?"

I had expected to hear from them, for in many cases I felt I had been there for them during their crises. But when the situation was reversed and I needed them, there was no contact.

As day after day passed with no contact from the friends whom I had expected to hear from, I found myself reviewing the list of absentee friends. As the faces of one after another walked across the stage of my mind, I asked myself over and over, *Why hasn't he called? I really thought I would hear from him!*

Since that time, I have come to realize that expectations are part of life, and they come in all different sizes and dimensions. Some are casual or superficial while others are much more involved. Expectations of an acquaintance come and go quickly. They are basically performance oriented and are limited to the realm of interaction with that individual. For example, the greatest expectation you have of the person who delivers your Sunday paper is that your paper arrives before you go out to retrieve it each Sunday morning. If it's there as you expected, you just pick it up and take it back inside where you eagerly page through your favorite section, followed by the remaining sections of the paper. You never consider how much time it took to assemble that Sunday morning masterpiece, section by section, or how early the delivery person had to get up to ensure that it was there exactly on time for you to enjoy at your discretion. Why? Because your expectations were met as soon as you stepped out the front door and saw the paper lying there as usual.

Those individuals whom I regarded as acquaintances met my expectations as soon as they said, "I'm so sorry to hear about your son, Steve" or "I just called to express my sympathy regarding the loss of David." But my expectations were much different toward those with whom I had a relationship.

Relational expectations are a different matter. These expectations are higher and more complex because of the deeper, more personal association with these individuals. I experienced firsthand the disappointment of these unmet expectations. My most vivid memories of this date back to the day after David's car crash.

I had returned from Cartersville, Georgia, on that day as I

shared in Chapter 1, after receiving the telephone call notifying me of the tragedy. When I arrived at our home, there were people everywhere. I must have been in a state of shock when I arrived, and the pain of David's death was overwhelming. I just wanted to be left alone with my thoughts.

The next day there were more people, coming and going all day long. Some were from the church, some from the neighborhood—mostly people whom I had seen at one time or another. Some of our relatives also arrived to be with us. Others from out of town called to express their sympathy. And their kindness and consideration were meaningful even though I was numb with pain and grief.

The third day brought more of the same—people stopping by or calling to tell us they were thinking of us or praying for us. There was a steady stream of visitors at the house all day long, and the telephone was seldom silent. Near the end of the day, the number of guests arriving started to dwindle, and the house grew quiet and still again. I was still dazed by David's passing, and the activity of our friends and loved ones coming and going had made for a full and somewhat tiring day.

As I sat down to rest and reflect on the day, I thought about the sea of faces that had visited our home in the last day or two, along with the many who had called. I felt their love, and it helped me deal with reality even though my heart was breaking. As I thought about my friends and how much it meant to have them there and feel their love, an old friend came to mind. *I haven't heard from him . . . I wonder why?* Almost immediately the face of another longtime acquaintance came to mind, followed by another. I hadn't heard from any of these men, and I was shocked. In fact, now that I thought about it, there were many individuals whom I had expected to call or contact me regarding David's death. But they had not.

Not hearing from them was unsettling for me. I was disappointed and hurt, perhaps even a little bitter that they hadn't made some effort to contact me. I couldn't believe that they didn't care enough to make a quick telephone call to ask how we were. How could they be so insensitive and uncaring?

Up to the time of David's tragic death, I always felt that I could depend on any one of my friends to help if something happened. I was certain that I could count on them, no matter what. But I wasn't aware of what my expectations really were regarding people. I had experienced disappointment from time to time as everyone does, but I never really understood just how subtle expectations can be or how easily I could be wounded by these false expectations.

It's almost as if you line your friends up in your mind and tell yourself what you expect from them. When someone doesn't live up to your expectations, which—by the way, are stored safely and secretly in the vault of your mind—you are devastated. If the situation persists, you may even become bitter toward them. That's what happened to me.

This may shock you, but I never struggled with bitterness toward the drunk driver of the car that took David's life, although I'm told many who lose a loved one in this way do. Perhaps I didn't face bitterness toward him because he, too, was killed in the crash, so I never had any contact with him following David's death. However, I did struggle with bitterness in the area of my expectations regarding my peers. I simply could not understand why they didn't contact me when I was hurting so badly.

I could not believe that these individuals didn't even bother to pick up the telephone and ask, "How are you doing, Steve?" Some of them were ministers who dealt with tragedy and death on a regular basis. In addition, they were my friends, and I expected them to know how much I needed them at a time like this. Yet most of my neighbors, whom I met after moving into this neighborhood only six months earlier, demonstrated more concern than some individuals whom I had known for half of my life.

As these thoughts were bombarding my mind, I heard that familiar still, small voice of the Lord whisper, "Steve, whom did you ever call when you heard about a tragedy? Where were you when your friends needed you?"

The reality of the question pierced through me like a sharp, gleaming spear. *No one . . . absolutely no one,* I thought. On a number of occasions I had heard of traumatic events and tragedies that my friends and former associates were facing. But I had never taken the time to contact them or let them know that I was thinking about them and praying for them.

"Who am I," I mused, "to be upset and bitter at my friends for not calling me when I have been guilty of the same thing?"

## YOU CAN DEPEND ON ME

I learned a valuable lesson through this experience—something that I had really always known and is even affirmed in Scripture. I had temporarily forgotten that "it is better to trust in the LORD / Than to put confidence in man" (Psalm 118:8).

It is likely that there will be individuals throughout your lifetime and mine who will do things that imitate or resemble friendship, but remember, "There is a friend who sticks closer than a brother" (Proverbs 18:24). That Friend is Jesus Christ! And no matter what comes your way, you can always depend on Him, for He is "Jesus Christ . . . the same yesterday, today, and forever" (Hebrews 13:8).

My struggles with unreal expectations and the disappointments that accompanied those struggles didn't end with my friends and associates. It extended to my family as well. I think I expected more from those who were close to me, especially after going through such a tragedy. For example, without ever discussing the matter with them, I just expected Pat and Tony to understand what I was going through and respond accordingly. I focused on *my* pain and *my* loss, showing little regard or concern for them or their feelings.

## WHAT NEXT?

The sense of loss that enveloped me eventually prompted a war with loneliness and fear. As C. S. Lewis once wrote in *A Grief Observed*, "I never knew that grief felt so like fear."[1] Fear is a natural component of grief; once you've experienced the death of a loved one, you *know* the world is not a safe place.

I began to wonder what I was going to lose next. I missed David, and I couldn't bear the thought of losing someone else. I can recall one occasion that really brought this fear to the forefront. Pat's parents had traveled from their home in Washington State to spend Christmas with us. Tony had made plans to stop by Gwen's house before dinner. They had been dating for a while, and we understood that he wanted to wish Gwen and her family a merry Christmas too.

Tony made us aware of his plans, reassuring us that he would be home in plenty of time for our holiday dinner. Pat cooked a beautiful meal, working diligently to make it very special as only she can do. The table was set and everything was ready, but Tony wasn't home yet. Pat and I, along with her parents, didn't want to start without Tony so we just waited. Thirty minutes went by, then an hour, then two. By now we were sitting at the table, just looking at each other, wondering where Tony could be.

Soon our concern turned to worry and dread. What could possibly have happened? Where was Tony? Had there been an accident? Had he been hurt, or worse? Where could he possibly be?

In the midst of our anxiety and worry, the kitchen door swung open, and Tony came strolling in with a big smile on his face.

I jumped to my feet and demanded to know where he had been and what had happened.

He said he had stopped by Gwen's house as planned. Before long, he and Gwen got into a conversation with her parents. They talked about this and that—nothing of any real significance. "We were having such a good time, I completely forgot about the time. When I finally noticed what time it was, I hurried home so you wouldn't worry." Then he added, "I was in such a hurry that I didn't even take time to call. I knew that you would be waiting for me."

As I look back on that evening now, I realize that if this same situation had happened before David's death, it would have affected me in a totally different way. I would have seen Tony's late arrival for what it was—a delay. I would not have been worried or affected as deeply as I was. But because David was gone, anxiety and fear had rolled in on me and overwhelmed me temporarily. The longer I waited for Tony to come home that night, the more fearful I became that some tragedy had happened to him. I felt that I had lost so much when David was taken from us, and I didn't want to have anything else stolen away.

Our private expectations of one another, along with our reluctance to talk about what we were feeling, contributed to some of the worry and anxiety we encountered in the months following David's death. That worry led to some painful experiences such as the one I just described.

I once heard someone say that the majority of what we worry about never comes to pass. That is true. So many of the concerns and worries I faced after losing David were based on my fear of losing another loved one. Not until I was able to identify that fear of loss and face it did I begin to realize some relief from this kind of anxiety. A portion of facing it entailed having the courage to verbalize some of my feelings. It wasn't easy at first because I had grown accustomed to hiding my feelings. As a family, we finally had to come to a place where we talked more openly about situations like the one I mentioned above, discussing what we could have done to ease the concern and avoid unnecessary worry. As we were able to talk about these emotions we had faced in our times of private mourning, we began to rebuild our lives, our traditions, and to look toward a brighter tomorrow, individually and as a family.

## DOES ANYBODY CARE?

Expectation and disappointment can be a trap for the individual who is grieving. If you're not discerning, it can be a permanent trap!

In the days and weeks that followed David's death, I asked

this question on many occasions: "Does anybody care?" My question was prompted by the loneliness I experienced day after day as I tried to come to grips with David's death and the abandonment I felt when the expectations I had of my longtime friends were not met.

When I finally stopped looking to my "friends" and began looking at myself, I realized that I had probably been guilty of bringing the same types of disappointments to many of my friends at one time or another. It was when I started to see myself in a proper light that I came to a most amazing realization: some of my friends really did care. Their love and concern were clearly demonstrated in many different ways—ways much different from what my expectations had allowed for.

The following list is in no way all-inclusive, but it reflects some of the ways individuals showed their love and concern toward me. Their gestures of kindness were practical and yet so helpful to Pat and me at a time when we felt so helpless. Along with the do's, I've included a few things to avoid. Having been the recipient of many kind, considerate acts, I'm providing this sample listing to share some of the best ways I know of to show love and concern for grieving friends and loved ones.

*Call or stop by as soon as possible.* Get in touch with the bereaved and express your condolences and your concern for the survivors. Your kind words, a card, flowers, a telephone call, telegram, or some form of contact helps immensely. Any form of communication that demonstrates your concern and awareness of the loss will be meaningful and will help strengthen a grieving person in his or her time of sorrow and loss.

*Express your love in a practical way.* Offer to run errands (i.e., taking clothes to the cleaners, making a trip to the grocery store, etc.) or just be there to answer the telephone. Offer to help the bereaved individual prepare for out-of-town relatives who may be arriving for the funeral. Prepare a meal for the loved ones left behind. Make something that can be nibbled at, reheated, or refrigerated easily, and avoid recipes that are extremely spicy or spoil easily.

Day after day many loving, caring people stopped by our house when we lost David. In fact, so many people came to our house that one of our neighbors graciously moved some of their furniture into our home so friends and relatives dropping by would have a place to sit.

Hundreds of people came to our home to express their love and sympathy. Those days were a blur to me; sometimes I noticed who was there, sometimes I didn't. Many who came by graciously brought casseroles, cakes, and other easy-to-serve food items. Pat, Tony, and I had no appetite to speak of, and mealtime was not a part of our schedule during the first few days. We felt as if our lives had been turned upside down and shaken, and food was not on our list of priorities then.

But when someone came by who had taken the time to prepare something for us, we felt their love and concern, both through their visit and through the time they had spent lovingly preparing something to help us through a most difficult time. Remember, individuals who are mourning the loss of a loved one may be totally preoccupied with their pain and with their immediate responsibilities. At times they may have to be reminded to eat or rest and will respond to being taken care of.

*Don't be afraid to give the mourner a hug.* Loneliness is a constant foe for the individual who has lost a loved one. The touch of a hand can speak volumes and often reminds the one who is grieving that someone cares and that they are not alone.

*Remember grieving friends during the holidays.* Many individuals become depressed during the Christmas and New Year holidays. Although they may have other family and you may not think of them as being alone, holidays like Christmas can accentuate the absence of a deceased loved one.

After David's death, a particularly difficult time for me began prior to the Christmas holidays and continued until February. Why? Because Christmas had always been a special family time that we looked forward to and February was the month of David's birthday.

Beginning with Christmas 1986, the holidays have continued to be a difficult time of year for me. Although the difficulties that I first experienced have eased some, I still have times in which the degree to which I miss David is overwhelming. Because of the struggles during holidays of years gone by, I can now anticipate the arrival of this time of year and prepare myself through prayer and by staying focused. This has helped me greatly, and the Lord has truly sustained me as I have called upon Him for help and strength.

*If at all possible, attend the funeral.* Whether or not your presence at the funeral is acknowledged immediately, know that you have made a difference by being there. It is of great help to know that someone else shares your sense of loss and grief. The fact that you were there may be more important to the bereaved in the days and weeks that follow than at the time of the actual funeral.

When Pat, Tony, and I walked through the doors of the church at David's memorial service, we each were so filled with emotion. As I discussed in Chapter 2, Pat was standing on one side of me, and Tony was on the other. Together, they locked their arms behind me and helped me inch my way down the aisle. That day was an extremely emotional day, and I didn't stop to take attendance or look at every face. But the fact that the church was filled to capacity did help to strengthen me.

On many occasions since that day I have thought about how many people came to that service to say good-bye to David. To know that my son had touched so many lives in his brief sixteen-year life was a source of comfort for me, and I felt proud to have a son who had made such an impact on so many lives in such a short time.

*Don't forget about the bereaved individual when you drive away from the cemetery.* It is likely that they may need you most during the days and weeks after the funeral is over.

As I mentioned earlier, our house was jammed with people during the days before David's memorial service. Friends dropped by and out-of-town family members came to be with us. Telegrams arrived, and the phone rang constantly. People brought food over and offered their help wherever they could. The love of all these wonderful people strengthened us as we prepared to say our final farewells to David.

But after the funeral and the burial service, loneliness and grief took on a new dimension for Pat and me. The people who surrounded us during those first few days after the crash were no longer there. They had returned to their families, jobs, and responsibilities. We were left alone to discover what we had left.

We did our best to return to normal, but life does not automatically go back to normal, for nothing will ever be the same again. When you lose a loved one, someone close to your heart has been permanently removed from your life. There is no way to instantaneously return to what has been the norm for you. Only time will grant you the ability to accept that loss and go on in spite of it. Time does not bring healing; it simply gives you the ability to heal. Only God can bring healing to a grieving heart.

I'm grateful for some of our very close friends who were a source of great strength to us after the funeral. From time to time they would call and check on us. Some called frequently; others called after a month or two, and then at regular intervals after that. If you genuinely care about someone who has suffered a loss through the death of a loved one, take time to tell them. Get a regular status report, and in so doing, you will be reminding them just how important they are to you. Your regular contact with them will also let them know that they are not alone.

*Be a good listener.* Although I didn't feel much like talking to anyone (and often did what I could to avoid conversation during those days), talking about David and how much I missed him did help. Although he was physically gone from us, talking about him helped me deal with some of the pain. His departure from our home and from our lives was unexpected and tragic. Through our shared experiences during his sixteen years of life, timeless memories were made. Being able to talk about David and reminisce about those memories helped bring healing to my life.

*Don't say things like "I know how you feel" if you have never experienced the loss of a close loved one.* Every relationship in life is unique, with special memories, traditions, and hopes for the future. No matter how deeply you may empathize with the emotional pain of the bereaved, you most likely do not know how they feel at that moment.

*Don't offer your personal opinions or spiritual insights.* Hearing someone's speculation about the whys when you are mourning the loss of a loved one is the last thing you want or need.

Most of the individuals who came to our home to express their sympathy after David's death were wonderful, caring people. But I can remember a few rare cases who were a total turnoff. They offered not only their condolences, but also their unsolicited opinions on why David had been taken from us, what God's plan was in all this, and on and on. They were by no means comforting, and to be honest, I wanted to turn around and run from them. Their visits were memorable, but not necessarily in a positive way.

*Say or do something!* If you really care about the individual who has lost a loved one, take time to call and express your love to them.

Nearly two years after David's death I came face-to-face with a pastor whom I had expected to hear from around the time of the funeral. During our brief conversation that day, I asked him why he had never called after David's death. His answer stunned me. He said, "Well, Steve, I was going through a hard time then, and I just didn't know what to say." I told him it wouldn't have mattered what he said, if only he had called!

This is true for many individuals who don't know what to say to someone who has lost a loved one. Let me make a suggestion. If you do not live near the bereaved individual, a telephone call can successfully communicate your love and concern. Just calling to let a grieving man or woman know that you are there and that you are thinking about them is all that is necessary. What you say is not nearly as important as just making contact with them to let them know that you care.

*Stay in contact.* One gentleman named Max Morris understood how important this was, and his concern made such an impact on me. He was faithful to call me every year around the date of David's death. His call was never lengthy, but hearing from him at that time of the year made such a difference for me. Year after year he called to say, "I'm thinking of you today. How are you doing?"

At the writing of this book it has been ten years since David's death, and Max never forgets. He still calls or writes or leaves a brief message every year around the anniversary of David's death just to check up on us as a family.

Each year as July 27 approaches, an invisible shadow clouds my life as I remember what happened on that date that changed my life forever. But Max's gentle touch on my life through his annual telephone call, saying, "I'm thinking of you today," has helped to make each year brighter. He has touched my life in a very special way, and I know he cares.

*Allow the bereaved person to grieve in their own way.* Grieving is part of the healing process. If people close to you have lost a loved one, allow them to grieve in their own way. That's what Curt and Mavis Lawson did for Pat and me. Whether we were having a good day or a difficult day, as we tried to cope with our pain, they were always there for us. We knew that they cared about us, and we could count on them. If it hadn't been for them, I don't think we would have made it through this difficult time in our lives. When there seemed to be no way out of our dark tunnel of grief, their love and support gave us strength for the day. And somehow we knew that somewhere up ahead, there was a brighter tomorrow.

## FROM THE HEART

The list I provided in this chapter represents some of the ways in which our friends and loved ones showed their love and support to us as individuals and as a family when we so desperately needed it. It is not intended to be an exhaustive list, for there are many other things that you can do to help someone through a time of grief and loss.

Remember: a list of suggestions is not nearly as important as love, for when you love someone and care about them and the pain they feel, you don't need a list to guide you—just follow your heart.

## CHAPTER 7

# GOOD DAYS, BAD DAYS

*U*ntil July 27, 1986, calendars at the Brock house recorded every series of seven days in the same way: Sunday, Monday, Tuesday, Wednesday, Thursday, Friday, and Saturday. But when the sun rose and attempted to shine on my dark, gloomy world on July 28, my entire point of reference had suddenly changed. It didn't matter any longer what day of the week the calendar said it was. For me it was either a good day or a bad day—and the majority were bad!

As I discussed in a previous chapter, most of my waking hours following David's tragic death were spent in lonely emotional exile. I was consumed with the questions of "if only" and "why" and I was determined to find the answers.

During this time Pat didn't say much about what she was going through, either, and I didn't really ask. I knew she was dealing with her grief in her own way. I was wandering aimlessly through my wilderness of woe, preoccupied primarily with my questions, and this lonely trek sapped all my strength. At times it was all I could do to face another day.

When I wasn't totally consumed with my own pain, I did notice that Pat was seldom idle; she was constantly working or busy doing something. But I reasoned that she had always been a very motivated, aggressive person—especially in matters of responsibility—so I didn't think it particularly strange that she was absorbed in her work.

However, several years after David's death I came upon some information that was very enlightening and helped me understand Pat more. I discovered that it is quite normal for highly motivated individuals like Pat, who suffer a loss of such magnitude as she did, to mask their pain by becoming workaholics. By keeping the mind busy all or most of the time, there is essentially no time left for a grieving individual to think about the present, reflect on the past, or deal with the uncertainty of the future. By pouring themselves totally into their work and investing nearly all their energy in each project, by the time this type of individual falls into bed at night, they are so exhausted that they just sink into the arms of blissful sleep.

## WHAT ABOUT TONY?

Sandwiched somewhere between Pat's workaholic behavior and my lonely, self-exiled introspection was Tony, our seventeen-year-old son. He was doing his best to cope with his own grief, but it was very difficult for him because he basically had no one to turn to.

At the time I didn't realize the magnitude of what Tony was dealing with. Although we all lived together in the same house, we were more like casual acquaintances than a family. I can see now that we were each trying to spare one another from the sadness and sense of loss that we struggled with individually. We were each trying to handle our pain in our own way, loving one another so much that we tried to hide our feelings in order to make each other more comfortable. In so doing, however, we seldom talked about our feelings because it was still too painful. But sadly, our silence only helped to reinforce the invisible walls that we had unknowingly built with exacting perfection.

## TONY'S TRIALS

David's death was a traumatic experience for our entire family, but the challenges Tony faced were different from those that Pat and I encountered. One of the things Tony had to deal with was the overnight transition from sibling to only child! As I shared in an earlier chapter, he said good-bye to his brother on Saturday afternoon after our golf game and by the next day, he was an only child!

As you'll remember from Chapter 1, Tony was there with me in Cartersville when I got the telephone call about David's car wreck. Having him there was a great comfort for me, but I know it wasn't easy for him. You see, before we lost David, our family was very close. We enjoyed the same things, shared common goals in life, and did nearly everything together. When we worked, we worked hard. When we played and relaxed, we did that with the same intensity. Whenever we faced difficulties, we faced them together, drawing strength and courage from one another.

But when that telephone call came, our stable family unit was altered. First of all, we were not physically together. Tony and I were away for the weekend in unfamiliar surroundings, Pat was home alone in Hamilton, and David was gone forever!

With David's abrupt exit from our lives, everything was shaken and thrown into total upheaval. Suddenly we were adrift on a raging sea, and the emotional waves on those uncharted waters seemed ready and waiting to drown us in grief.

## SOMEONE TO LEAN ON

As I look back on those days now, I can see how brave Tony was at the age of only seventeen and in the face of so much uncertainty. I remember how strong he was that day as we flew back to Hamilton and also during the long, empty days that preceded the funeral. And when I walked into the church that day for the funeral, flanked by Pat on one side and Tony on the other, I leaned on him—physically and emotionally. Seeing that casket at the front of the church made my knees so weak I couldn't even walk. I still don't know if I could have made it down that long aisle without his help. But I didn't have to consider that possibility, for Tony was there beside me, just as he had been each step of the way since the terrible news first came.

## SUFFERING IN SILENCE

As time passed, Pat and I continued to internalize much of our pain, saying very little about what we were feeling. I've been told that children respond to pain and loss in much the same way parents grieve. That was certainly true of Tony. Pat quietly worked away the hours, busying herself as long as possible each and every day. Day after day I sat silently, pondering the reasons for this tragedy that had altered our lives. I focused on what I had lost rather than recognizing what I still had. I was so preoccupied with *my* questions and *my* pain that I failed to notice the agony and suffering of those around me whom I loved most, Pat and Tony.

With Pat totally absorbed in her work and me completely consumed with my thoughts, questions, and relentless grief, Tony had no one to turn to. With David gone and neither Pat nor me to talk to, Tony wasn't just an only child—he was more like an orphan. By default he, too, was forced to suffer in silence.

## NO ONE TO TALK TO

Silence can be a terrible prison, one that holds you captive with invincible perfection. Once you have been locked up in its silent vacuum, it's nearly impossible to escape from its hopeless, impenetrable walls.

Not long after the funeral, Tony said, "Everybody was here, and then all of a sudden, nobody was!" In the days immediately following the death of a loved one, a number of people often visit or call, bring food, or express their love and concern in some tangible way, including attending the funeral. But after the funeral is over, support can fade alarmingly fast for there is no book of etiquette that outlines the proper response for the friends of those who are grieving. Consequently, family and friends are left to draw their own conclusions, often with no obvious indicators from the bereaved.

When Tony first made the statement, I thought he was referring to the friends and relatives who had come to be with us for the funeral. So many individuals who had touched our lives in some way through the years had come to show their love and support during this time. Just knowing that they cared helped so much, even in the midst of our grief.

Their love, along with the mandatory details and preburial decisions Pat and I were forced to take care of, kept us busy and focused. We spent most of our energy just dealing with each day's responsibilities, sometimes at the expense of Tony's needs.

Some people marveled at how we managed to deal with our traumatic and tragic loss during this time, commenting on our strength to go through such a difficult experience. Little did they know that what they mistook for strength was really shock! We were numb with pain because David had been taken from us so suddenly, and we were barely existing.

Recently while reading a pamphlet on the topic of grief produced by MADD (Mothers Against Drunk Driving), I came across the following:

> During this time, people may have commented on how "strong" you were. One of the saddest parts of trauma is that people assume you are strong when you really are in shock. You may appear strong, but you feel like a mechanical robot. When the shock wears off and you desperately need your friends, they have resumed life as usual, believing that you are doing fine.[1]

I can relate so well to this because that's exactly what happened to us. When Tony made his comment about everyone being here and then suddenly disappearing, I thought he was just referring to the sudden arrival and departure of our out-of-town friends and relatives. But now as I reflect on everything that was going on inside the silent world of the Brock house, I'm not so sure.

## SCHOOL DAYS, SCHOOL DAYS

David's death occurred in late July, so four or five weeks after the funeral, the fall term of school started. It was Tony's senior year and should have been one of the highlights of his high school experience. But things were different that year. From the first morning when he ate breakfast alone to when he got into his car and drove the short distance to school alone—over and over, Tony was reminded of how different life was.

Children who have experienced the loss of a brother or sister in death face many difficulties that adults never encounter. They face uncomfortable situations with their peers and others they come in contact with. That's what happened to Tony. And to make matters worse, some of the students didn't even know about the tragedy that had occurred that summer.

Tony and David were almost always seen together, especially at school, because whenever possible, David was close behind Tony. When Tony returned to school that fall, he had a very awkward experience the first day. As he was walking down a corridor of the school, someone shouted a greeting to him. Then he added, "Hey, Tony, where's David? I haven't seen him all day!"

Tony paused and waited for the student to approach. "You . . . uh . . . don't know what happened this summer? . . . You didn't hear about the accident?" Tony began. And in somber tones he proceeded to explain why David wasn't at school that day and would never be there again.

## LOOKING FOR COMFORT

This was a hard time for all of us because we were each looking for comfort, but I think it must have been a little harder for Tony. Pat and I had each other, although we really didn't talk much about our feelings or our pain. From what I could gather, Tony seemed to be doing OK now that school had resumed, even though his absentee rate for the year was almost a day a week. He seemed to stay busy enough with school, and he didn't say much about David anymore. However, if I had taken the time to ask how he was doing, I would have made a startling discovery.

In his own way, Tony was trying his best to deal with losing his brother, and he didn't want to say much because he saw what a rough time Pat and I were having. So, with no one to console him, Tony began looking elsewhere for solace. It didn't take him long to find something to comfort him, but because I was trapped by my own agony, I was oblivious to the choice he had made. In fact, I didn't learn about his newfound "companion" until the following February.

## THE MEMORIAL TOURNAMENT

During the years I served as pastor of the church in Hamilton, the church had helped to start a citywide church basketball league. The teenagers and young adults from the various churches made up the teams and had a great deal of fun competing against one another.

During the basketball season immediately following David's death, the church league decided to hold their first and only memorial basketball tournament—the David Brock Memorial Tournament—in honor of my son. Although the tournament was in David's honor, I couldn't make myself attend, but Tony did.

I was at home watching television by myself that evening. At one point I noticed the time and determined that the game must be over by now. Tony wasn't home yet, but I didn't think much about it because, in Tony's opinion, curfews were set to be broken. He was a notorious "curfew pusher." He would do everything in his power to stay out with his friends until the last possible minute before his curfew, which was usually midnight. He always arrived just in time!

But that night was not the norm by any stretch of the imagination. After watching the news, I made my way to the kitchen. I found Pat sitting at our kitchen table, which is situated directly in front of a large bay window facing the street. I sat down and made small talk for a few minutes. About 10:30 P.M. I saw some headlights go past the house. I didn't think anything of it until the lights went by again. Not long after, the headlights passed our house a third time, followed by some commotion nearby at one of the neighbor's homes. Just minutes after the disturbance, I heard someone come in through the basement entrance. The noise startled me, so I looked at my watch.

*Ten-thirty! Tony? Impossible! Something must be wrong with my watch!* I thought. I verified the time and started downstairs to investigate. Tony was unusually early! But I knew it had to be Tony—who else could it be?

As I reached the basement of our home, I heard something coming from the bathroom. I started in that direction, still listening carefully. I paused in the hallway outside the basement bathroom for a moment. It sounded as if water was running. "Tony," I said, "is everything all right? What are you doing home so early?"

The sound of running water coming from the bathroom stopped almost immediately as I called out to Tony. Then I heard the familiar sound of the doorknob turning, and the door slowly began to open, revealing Tony.

That was when I met Tony's new "friend." As soon as I got near him, the smell of alcohol came wafting toward me. I couldn't believe it—Tony was drunk!

Instantly a flurry of emotions converged upon me—anger, concern, worry, confusion, frustration—and any other emotion that could possibly enhance the already explosive situation.

After the initial shock wore off and I calmed down, Tony and I sat down to talk. I began by asking him what had happened to make him surrender to the same enemy that had taken his brother from us. That's when I got the first glimpse of the "other" Tony.

## WHERE'S THE REAL TONY?

"I'm not really who you think I am, Dad," Tony began. "I've tried to be strong and make it—but it's been a tough year.

Having people at school ask about David is too much to handle, and then trying to live like everything is normal when it's not—it's just too hard!"

Tony paused for a moment to collect his thoughts before continuing. "Last July when David died, I wasn't what you thought I was. I wasn't really living for the Lord. You didn't know it, but I had been drinking off and on during the whole summer. I wasn't living like you and Mom have always taught me. Some of my friends were drinking, so I thought I'd try it too.

"After David was taken from us, I went running back to the Lord because of the terrible circumstances—not because I wanted Him to be the Lord of my life. But that didn't even last two months. The awful reality of everything hit me about three or four months later, and I just couldn't cope with David's death. Every day that I went to school I was reminded in some way about David. Kids would ask questions, and I wasn't strong enough spiritually to handle everything, so I just started drinking again—and with a bunch of kids from the church! We all thought we were indestructible and could handle the alcohol. Besides, it seemed to help me forget how much I missed David.

"Our team won the game tonight at the tournament, so a bunch of us went out to celebrate. We went to a restaurant where we usually go when we want to have a good time. They never check our IDs either.

"We got something to eat and ordered some beer. In fact, we had all the beer we wanted. But I wasn't really having a very good time. After all, we were celebrating our victory at a tournament held in honor of my brother who is dead! I thought, *What's to celebrate?* So I decided to come home.

"As I came up the hill in front of the house, I glanced at the clock. I couldn't believe that it was only 10:30! I was shocked because I never come home this early!

"By the time I got to the top of the hill, I realized that I must be drunk, too, because I was having a hard time controlling the car. And then when I saw the house, I asked myself, *What are you doing? You can't walk into your home with alcohol on your breath.*" Tony paused a moment and then continued. "You see, Dad, I've learned how to live such a hypocritical lifestyle. Whenever I came home drunk before, I would chew gum or drink coffee to mask the smell of the alcohol. And it worked, because you and Mom never picked up on it. Tonight I was shocked that I got so close to the house and hadn't thought about doing anything that I normally do to cover up the smell.

"As I was thinking about how I could deceive you again and cover up the smell of the beer, I took a good look at myself. I didn't like what I saw, and I couldn't believe what I had become. I felt like the prodigal son, wallowing around in the pig slop. That's when I started driving around the block. I was trying to figure out what to do. I knew I should let this smell wear off, and I had to regain control of my faculties before I came home."

I just sat there on the couch beside Tony, taking in everything he was saying. Tony just kept talking, as if some valve had been loosened and the pressure was being released as the words tumbled out of his mouth.

"That's when I came up with a plan," Tony continued. "I decided that I would drive around the neighborhood to sober up. I went by the house once, and I saw you and Mom sitting at the kitchen table. I didn't know if you had seen me or not, and I wasn't thinking very clear at that moment. So I drove around the block again. After the second or third time I went around the block, I was certain that you knew it was me. I decided to go around the block one more time before I came home.

"While I was making my final lap, I took a corner too quickly, lost control of the car, and ran into a neighbor's mailbox—the one around the corner with the big rocks cemented to the base. It all happened so fast. I saw the mailbox suddenly appear in front of me, then I saw it go flying up over the car. And when I checked, I thought I was all right. That's when I got out of the car to see if there was any damage. I couldn't believe my eyes! The rocks that had been around the bottom of the mailbox were the only thing left there. The mailbox was totally gone, and apparently the car hit the rocks because it looked like they tore out the whole middle section of the car! The car really looked bad, and there was oil pouring out everywhere. All I could think of was, *I've got to get this car home fast,* so I got back into the car and managed to pull the car under the carport.

"I pulled in, parked the car, and just sat there in the darkness. I thought, *I must be dreaming. After all, I'm not a bad person. How could this actually be happening to me?* All I wanted to do tonight was celebrate a little with some of my friends. I was hoping against all hope that it was a dream, but when I opened the car door and stepped out, I heard a splash and felt the oil under my shoe as my foot hit the ground. The carport floor was full of oil. I could smell the oil, too, even in my drunken state. And that's when I knew it was all real.

"I came in the house through the basement door as quietly as possible, but you must have heard me close the door. I went to the bathroom to splash some cold water on my face—that's all I could think of to try to sober up a little. That's about the time I heard your knock on the outside of the bathroom door. I was already beating myself up for being so stupid—for getting drunk and for wrecking the car. I didn't really want to open the door because I didn't know what would happen . . . I didn't know what you would do . . ."

Tony turned toward me and looked me straight in the eyes as he said, "Dad, it's been a terrible night. After I was dumb enough to come home drunk, I destroyed the neighbor's mailbox and wrecked the car. I didn't know what to do or where to go . . . so I just came home . . ."

"I'm glad you did, son," I said as I put my arms around him. "I'm glad you did."

## CHAPTER 8

# TONY'S TURNING POINT

Seven months had passed since David's senseless death. In a moment's time my world had come crashing down on me, and I felt as if my life had been reduced to shattered rubble.

That February night following the David Brock Memorial Basketball Tournament, I wondered what else was going to happen. Tony had come home drunk and had nearly destroyed the car on his way home. As I sat there listening to Tony trying to pronounce each slurred word in his drunken stupor, strong emotions flourished within me. I loved him so much, and I wanted to listen to everything he had to say. But the smell of the alcohol on his breath permeated the room and reminded me of the enemy that had stolen David from us. The thought of Tony succumbing to any of that enemy's cunning ways was unbearable.

I looked at him sitting next to me on the couch. He had stopped talking for a moment as he sat there and just let me love him. As he began to speak again, he shared a most remarkable revelation with me.

## THE REVELATION

"Dad, I realized something tonight. I was just trying to get the car home safe, and I almost didn't make it. The car looks pretty bad, but it could have been so much worse. I could have been hurt, too, or worse yet, I could have hurt someone else.

"The guy that crashed into David didn't walk out the door that evening planning to kill himself and someone else. He was only nineteen years old and thought he was just going out to have a good time. I don't know for sure, but I think he might have been a young guy hurting, too, like I was tonight. As much as I love playing basketball and winning, I was really hurting tonight. I was all torn up. Our team won the game. But the game we won was at the David Brock Memorial Tournament—a tournament to honor the memory of my brother who's dead!

"I was really dumb to drive while I was drunk tonight. Fortunately, I only hit a mailbox instead of a family, a brother, a mom, or a dad. And I didn't take my life in the process like the guy who hit David . . ."

Tony hesitated for a moment, as if pondering something. Then he said, "Dad, you know . . . it's really true."

"What, son—what's true?" I asked.

"It's like I've heard you say: the thing you hate sometimes happens to you; the devil makes you the very thing you hate. The best way for the devil to get at you, Mom, and me was to get me with alcohol, and I was dumb enough to fall into his trap!

"I was David's big brother, but I wasn't strong like he was. David didn't care what his peers thought; he was very secure in who he was. He knew what he wanted and waited for it. But it was harder for me. When some of my friends started drinking, I wanted to fit in so much that I joined in and drank too. I should have known better, and somewhere deep inside, I guess I did, especially after David was gone. But I wanted to fit in and be accepted.

"Things have happened that should have made me realize where this road was headed, but I didn't pay attention. I never heard the wake-up call. Remember when my two front teeth got knocked out at that party?"

I nodded affirmatively, remembering the incident all too well as Tony continued.

"When that guy who was high on alcohol and steroids jumped on my back at that party and knocked out my two front teeth, I should have run for my life. But I didn't. I just kept trying to fit in with my friends, and they liked going to those kinds of places. After David died, you would have thought I'd never turn to alcohol again, even though I had been drinking some before the car crash. I did get straightened out for a little while, but the pain of losing David just kept getting worse, and my friends kept asking me to go drinking with them. Finally I was hurting so bad, I said yes to my friends, and before long I was drinking again. The alcohol seemed to help me forget some of the pain, but that was a real lie. The drinking didn't help anything.

"I've been trying to handle losing my brother and deal with the questions and stuff at school about David. And then seeing you and Mom hurting so . . . I just couldn't handle it. The alcohol didn't really change anything, but it eased the pain just a little, and it was a relief not to hurt so much, even if it was only for a little while!"

## A GLIMPSE OF MY SON

Tony and I talked for several hours that night—until nearly 4:00 A.M. Tony just kept pouring his heart out to me, and I sat there beside him, listening and loving him.

That was probably the first time in seven months that we had a real heart-to-heart talk. As I listened, I caught a glimpse of my son that had gone unnoticed until now. I saw a wounded, hurting young man, so fragile and desperate to be understood—not the Tony I had leaned on the day of the funeral just months before. My heart broke for him and all the agony he had experienced, agony that he had tried to keep locked securely inside.

I hugged Tony tight that night, and as I did, I thanked the Lord for him. I knew he must have really been hurting to turn to alcohol, especially since it was alcohol and a drunk driver that had taken David from us. And I was angry at the devil for laying such a devious trap for him.

## COME WITH ME, SON

It was getting late, and Tony looked so tired. As our lengthy conversation came to some temporary resolve, I said, "Tony, I'm leaving for Louisville around 7:00 A.M. I'm scheduled to preach there. I want you to come with me."

"Sure, Dad," Tony responded in his dazed condition. "I'll go along."

"We don't have long to sleep, son, so let's get some rest."

"OK, Dad," Tony said as he made his way to his room. As he was walking away, he paused, turned back toward me, and said, "Thanks, Dad."

## TONY'S TRANSFORMATION

That day in Louisville was one of the highlights of my life. Nothing could have been more dynamic or fulfilling for me as far as ministry goes. If I had visited all seven wonders of the world simultaneously, I couldn't have been more ecstatic. It was definitely a day I will never forget!

Now, I don't remember much of what I said in my sermon that morning, for I must admit, I was emotionally and physically exhausted from the night before. The three-hour drive to Louisville that morning had only added to my weariness. But when I gave the invitation at the close of the service, inviting those who wanted to surrender their lives completely to Jesus Christ to come forward, Tony was the first one to respond. Others followed closely behind.

As I watched him walk down to the front of the church that morning, I knew that he was serious from the look on his face. He was determined and desperate, and he wanted Jesus Christ to transform his life completely.

Years later Tony admitted that he didn't remember what I preached about that morning either. He said he had made a decision long before I began my message that it really didn't matter if I preached well or poorly that day. He knew from past experience that I would close my message with an altar call, and he had already decided that he was going to that altar when the invitation was given.

The prayer he prayed that morning was the beginning of a glorious transformation in Tony's life. There was no emotional display on his part or mine. I didn't recognize him publicly or rush to his side to pray with him that day. I felt deep inside that this was a holy moment between him and God.

I stood there watching as he prayed quietly. I didn't hear his prayer audibly, but it didn't matter what words he chose because the determined look on his face told me that he meant business and his heart was reaching God's heart.

I'll never forget that morning. From the moment Tony said amen, he was different—he was transformed—he was changed!

But as I look back on that day, so was I.

## A REASON TO LOOK TOWARD THE FUTURE

Following the service, we packed up and started for home. As we made the three-hour return trip we talked about a number of things, including the future. I told Tony that I wanted him to start going with me on the weekends whenever he could. He quickly agreed and said he would like that.

Little by little, he began to join me more often on the weekend ministry trips. He would help at the tape table or wherever he was needed. From time to time, he would also share a brief testimony of how his life had been transformed.

As the months passed, we talked more and spent more time together. This included some weekends when we would go to minister at a church together. During this time, I watched him grow spiritually. He began to make wise choices, spending more time with people whom he knew would not pull him away from the Lord. It seemed that he was becoming stronger in his walk with the Lord, along with his ability to say no to temptation. I was thrilled to see this growth in him.

In the midst of this, I didn't realize just how close the tempter was lurking, and I didn't learn of one such incident until several years later.

## OLD FRIENDS

Approximately two months after Tony's transformation in Louisville, he decided to go out with some of his old friends. He was worried about them because he suspected that they were still involved in some of the same old activities he had indulged in with them. His changed lifestyle and our weekend ministry trips had not allowed much time for him to be around them. He had missed being with his friends, and since some of them were "church kids," he decided to go.

He recently shared with me how much that night with old friends opened his eyes. His friends had planned a night of what they viewed as fun, including drinking and driving around town. Since Tony didn't plan to do any drinking, he volunteered to drive for his friends.

As Tony drove them around town, Tony noticed that they talked about the same old stuff while they tried to drink their troubles away and find happiness. Since Tony hadn't been with them very much, and because he wasn't drinking, he just drove while they talked.

As the conversation continued, Tony listened as the speech of one after another became so blurred and slurred that it was difficult to understand what they were saying. Suddenly from the backseat Tony heard one of his friends mumble these words: "Pull over . . . now! I'm going to be sick!"

"Yuck! Not in the car!" blurted out another voice.

Tony pulled the car over onto the side of the road and stopped. His friend in the backseat opened the door and almost fell out of the car as he hurried away in search of a place to relieve himself. He had only taken a step or two when Tony heard the familiar, gut-wrenching sound of someone throwing up, a sound that he had heard many times before in similar settings.

*What a disgusting sound,* Tony thought as his friend continued to throw up at the side of the road.

"That's where you were," the familiar, gentle voice of the Lord whispered to Tony as he observed his sick friend from the driver's seat. "You were confused and looking for something to make you happy. But true happiness is found in Me."

Proverbs 28:14 states, "Happy is the man who is always reverent, But he who hardens his heart will fall into calamity." Proverbs 3:13 says, "Happy is the man who finds wisdom, / And the man who gains understanding."

Ecclesiastes 7:12 states, "But the excellence of knowledge is that wisdom gives life to those who have it."

That evening as Tony watched his friends "have a good time," he began to understand the deceptive plan of the enemy and how close he had been to falling prey to that trap just a few months earlier. He thought he made a most amazing discovery on his own that night, but his praying mother was thanking God for a victory that had first been won in intercession. What Tony saw that night was really just a visual display of the enemy's battle plans for his life—battle plans that were doomed for failure when a praying mother joined the ranks!

## GOOD-BYE WORLD!

Today Tony looks back on that night as a real turning point in his life. The vivid reality of what alcohol had to offer was dramatically portrayed through his friend's "performance at the roadside theater." From that night on, Tony says he never had a problem with alcohol again. He no longer felt any need for the false sense of comfort it had once offered.

That night Tony discovered that the only true and lasting comfort available was found in the Lord Jesus and in His wonderful love. Tony made a decision to stand firm and rest in the comfort that he had found.

# CAMP MEETING '87

The following July I was scheduled to preach for "Youth Night" at the annual summer Church of God Camp Meeting. Since it was summertime and school was out, I asked Tony to join me and go along. He accepted.

Before we left home, I asked Tony if he would like to share a brief testimony about what he had gone through the last year, especially since it was "Youth Night." Since he had shared his testimony at some of my services in the past, he thought about it for only a moment and agreed.

## A DREAM COME TRUE

The auditorium was packed with teenagers and young adults that night, and the atmosphere was bustling with the energy and enthusiasm that are characteristic of massive youth meetings. As the service began and the music started, I couldn't help thinking about David. *If it hadn't been for that fatal crash a year ago,* I thought, *he might have been here with me tonight too.* Then I quickly glanced at Tony who was sitting nearby. I was thankful that I had Tony, and I was glad that he had come with me.

When the customary preliminaries such as congregational singing, special music, the offering, and special prayer had been completed, I was introduced as the speaker for the evening. The teenagers and young adults welcomed me with warm applause. When the applause had diminished enough for me to be heard, I began my message. The teenagers seated before me were a lively group, and it was easy to preach to them. My message led naturally into some of the problems Tony had experienced in the last year, so I included that as well. Then I introduced Tony and asked him to come and share his testimony for a few minutes.

Tony stepped up onto the platform and started to speak. As he shared his heart, the timid, shy Tony vanished before my eyes. I watched in amazement as he spoke with a boldness and authority I had never seen before. He told the teenagers how he had searched for answers in alcohol but had finally found everything he needed in Jesus.

Twenty minutes later Tony handed the microphone back to me and returned to his seat. As I accepted the microphone, I was dumbfounded! The two- to three-minute teenage testimony had become a twenty-minute sermon that challenged every teenager present to discover the answer to life—Jesus Christ!

I thought, *There's nothing more I can add.*

"Bow your heads, please," I said as I drew the microphone to my lips. I gave the same invitation that I had given that February morning in Louisville when Tony's life was so miraculously transformed.

That night at the Camp Meeting four hundred young people came forward to surrender their lives to Jesus Christ. As a minister of the gospel, it was overwhelming to see so many teenagers and young adults make a decision to start living 100 percent for Christ.

As a father, it was a dream come true! How thrilling it was for me to see Tony stand before that crowd and declare the gospel with such authority. I was so proud of him as he reminded his peers that they could achieve their dreams if they would say no to drugs and alcohol and yes to Jesus Christ. And my heart leaped for joy as I was able to realize a dream and minister with my son for the first time that night—but definitely not the last.

## WHEN THE SILENCE CEASES

It has been several years since David's home-going, and from time to time Pat, Tony, and I still discover new things about that time period in our lives—things we haven't really discussed or verbalized before.

For years we only acknowledged the tragedy, for it was an ever-present part of our lives. We avoided talking about it as much as possible because we only saw it as negative and as the vehicle that had stolen David away from us.

Over the years I have contemplated writing a book and sharing this story, but I just couldn't bring myself to do it until now. Why? The pain was too great, and discussing any of the details related to that time period in my life only emphasized the void I felt.

Finally, as we began to tear down the walls of silence that we had so carefully built around ourselves, we were able to start sharing our feelings more openly with one another. As we have opened up, we have begun to see things in a more positive light, and this has enhanced the healing process in each of our lives.

Tony recently shared a thought that underscores this. He was commenting on how grateful he is for his mother's prayers, especially during those months before Louisville. He said that he had just come to realize what great faith his mother had as she continued to let him go out and do the things he was doing. He knew that she was praying for him during this time of his life because he could feel her prayers.

"One night David left for church, and never came home," Tony observed. "What unshakable faith and trust she had in the Lord to let me go, knowing that I might not come back either. What confidence she had in God's ability to protect me from the devices of the enemy." Then he added, "Thank God for Mom and for her prayers!"

## SWEET RELIEF

What sweet relief we experienced as the years of darkness finally began to dissipate. At last we were able to take our eyes off the past and look beyond the moment with a sense of expectation.

As we opened our hearts to one another, we discovered a much deeper love than the superficial love that had caused us to remain silent. The gloom that had hovered over us was replaced by the light of God's love. In that glorious light of His love, we found hope for every tomorrow. And as the potential for a brighter tomorrow dawned on the horizon of our lives, it brought a gentle healing with it.

## CHAPTER 9

# MEET MY BROWN-EYED BEAUTY

W ho is that beautiful girl over there with the dark hair and beautiful brown eyes?"

That was the question that went through my mind the first time I laid eyes on Patsy Marie Marsh, now my wife of thirty years. From the first moment I saw her, I was drawn to her in a way that I had never experienced.

That introduction occurred on a Thursday evening, and by the following Tuesday I had asked her to marry me. (I would have proposed to her on Saturday, but I didn't want her to think I was impulsive!)

Let me tell you a little about how we met. My brother, Ronnie, and I had traveled to Memphis, Tennessee, to attend the General Assembly for the Church of God, a national convention. Although Ronnie and I were in our late teens at the time, we had been evangelizing for about two years throughout the Midwest and the eastern part of the States and we were very committed to our work for the Lord.

Even though my brother and I were young and single, we were very focused on our ministry. We had made a commitment not to date anyone at the churches while we held special services. Our busy schedule took us from city to city, and we basically had no time left for dating. However, the convention was another matter!

I can recall Ronnie's excitement as he thought about attending the convention. He was looking forward to the meetings, but he also made it very clear to me that since we were attending the convention and not conducting the services, he intended to make the most of the situation. In his eyes that meant a date for breakfast, a date for lunch, a date for dinner, and more, if possible! It sounded fine to me, too, so I agreed with him!

## HELLO, MY NAME IS STEVE

Not long after our arrival in Memphis, Ronnie and I were coming out of our hotel when to Ronnie's surprise, he saw a girl whom he had known in college coming out of the Peabody Hotel, which was located directly across the street from our hotel. He made his way across the street and approached the young lady. I followed along behind.

"Marilyn Kennedy," Ronnie said. "I haven't seen you since Lee College."

"Oh, hi, Ronnie," Marilyn responded. "It's been a while," she added with a quick smile.

"Yeah, it has," Ronnie said. By this time I was standing beside Ronnie, so I gave him a subtle nudge to remind him of my presence. "Oh, Marilyn, let me introduce my brother. This is Steve."

I said a courteous "Hello" as I glanced quickly at the beautiful young lady standing beside Marilyn.

Marilyn smiled warmly in my direction and said, "It's a pleasure to meet you, Steve." Then she turned slightly and gestured toward the young lady standing beside her. "This is Pat Marsh, my very best friend. She is from Yakima, Washington, and we came to Memphis to attend the convention together. Her father is a pastor in Washington, and they're here for the convention too."

"That's why we're here too," Ronnie added. He continued to renew old acquaintances with his college friend, while I took the opportunity to glance over at Pat again. As our eyes met, I noticed her beautiful brown eyes. Pat returned a friendly smile but said nothing.

When Ronnie and Marilyn had concluded their conversation, we excused ourselves and went our separate ways to get ready for the evening service.

By the time the evening service began, Ronnie had already arranged a double date for us with Marilyn and Pat. We planned to sit together at the service and go on the date afterward.

We met the girls before the service began and made our way to our seats. In just a few minutes the meeting began, but I must admit that I was somewhat oblivious to what was happening around me. I was captivated by the beautiful dark-haired, brown-eyed girl named Pat who sat beside me. Through the years Pat and I have reflected fondly upon that night, for it was the beginning of something wonderful.

Although Pat was very quiet that evening, I found out much later that she was thinking thoughts like, *This guy is so good-looking. He's got big, blue eyes and beautiful, wavy black hair. And although I've never heard of him, he seems to be very sincere about serving the Lord. He seems to have everything I ever wanted in someone. This is just too good to be true.*

## THE DATE AFTER CHURCH

When the church meeting was over, the four of us left for our date. Pat and I had a wonderful time together. We laughed and enjoyed good conversation. I even told a few jokes, which were warmly received (and laughed at) by Ronnie and the girls! As I got acquainted with Pat that night, I was intrigued by her. The more I learned about her, the more I wanted to know.

When the night was over and Ronnie and I had taken the girls back to their rooms, I was convinced that I had truly experienced "love at first sight." What I didn't know then, but would soon discover, was that Patsy Marie Marsh felt exactly the same way!

## BREAKFAST, LUNCH, AND DINNER

In the days that followed, Pat and I were inseparable. We shared breakfast, lunch, and dinner—and any other moment we could share between the scheduled meetings of the convention. As we got to know each other better, we discovered that we had so much in common. We liked the same things and shared many of the same interests. We even had the same goals in life. In Pat I saw someone who loved the Lord Jesus as I did and was deeply committed to serving Him. But at the same time, she was fun to be with. Every time we were together, we laughed and felt as though we had shared so much in such a short time.

By Saturday of that week it seemed as though Pat and I had known each other forever. We were attracted to one another in a way that we had never experienced before. I wanted to ask her to marry me that night, but I thought she might think I was some kind of nut. Even though the convention came to a close on Sunday, I convinced my brother that we should stay in Memphis a couple of days longer so I could spend some more time with Pat. He had been seeing Marilyn during this time, so he agreed very quickly.

Pat and I spent most of Monday and Tuesday together, and we had a wonderful time. The more we were together, the more we wanted to be together. I couldn't believe that we had known each other for only six days—it seemed like forever. And I certainly didn't want to face the future without this wonderful young lady by my side. So after knowing each other for just a few days, I asked Pat to marry me. To my delight, she accepted!

## HAVE I GOT NEWS FOR YOU!

As Ronnie and I were driving home from Memphis before going on to our next scheduled meetings, my thoughts were filled with Pat and the wonderful times we had shared during the previous week. I couldn't stop thinking about her, and I was thrilled that she had agreed to marry me!

As we drove along, I said, "Ronnie, I've got something to tell you."

"Really, Steve?" he said. "I've got something to tell you too. You go first."

"OK, Ronnie," I responded. "When you introduced me to Pat, that was the beginning of something wonderful. I believe that I've met my future wife, and I've asked her to marry me."

"And?" Ronnie said in a questioning tone.

"And she said yes!" I announced with a big smile.

"I'm happy for you, Steve," Ronnie said. Then he added, "Guess what?"

"What?" I asked.

"I've asked Marilyn to marry me, and she said yes!"

"You're kidding," I said in amazement.

"No. I asked her to marry me before we left Memphis, and she said yes!"

"Wow! I'm happy for you, Ronnie," I answered. Then I added, "What a convention!"

Ronnie just chuckled as we drove on toward home.

## GOD WORKS IN MYSTERIOUS WAYS

I firmly believe that when Pat and I met that Thursday evening it was not by chance, but by divine appointment. Psalm 37:4 says, "Delight yourself also in the LORD, / And He shall give you the desires of your heart." Later in that same Psalm we find these words in verse 23: "The steps of a good man are ordered by the LORD, / And He delights in his way."

I had committed my life, including my dating, to the Lord Jesus. As a young minister of the gospel, I was trusting the Lord with my future. In prayer I had asked the Lord to give me a mate who was committed to Him and His work. And that is exactly what began in Memphis.

Several months after the convention, I discovered that Pat had done exactly the same thing. Just prior to traveling to Memphis for that convention, Pat had a conversation with her father about God's will for her life. As an only child, she was very close to him and respected the wisdom he had to offer. She had asked, "How will I know when I meet the man God has for me?"

"Pat, if you will trust God for His perfect will for your life, He will bring it to pass. If the man God has for you lives on the other side of the United States, He'll bring the two of you together. Just pray and trust God."

Pat had been dating a young man steadily at the time she asked her father the question. Prayer had been a part of her life from the time she was very young. So, when her father suggested that she pray about God's will for her life, she did.

The young man had made plans to attend the national convention in Memphis, too, and had planned to meet Pat there. But when Pat arrived at the convention with her parents, she discovered that the young man she expected to see there didn't even show up. In just a matter of days, I believe God orchestrated our lives and brought us together—an answer to our prayers.

## THE LONG-DISTANCE COURTSHIP

Pat and I had enjoyed such glorious days together at the convention. When it ended, Ronnie and I returned to our service schedule. I loved the ministry Ronnie and I had together, and as I mentioned before, we were very committed to the work of the Lord. However as time passed, I missed Pat's companionship, which I had experienced for such a short time in Memphis. We had shared so much during that week at the convention, but it seemed that we had so much more to say to one another.

Pat and I stayed in contact by telephone and by correspondence, but a long-distance courtship is not the same. It can also be very expensive!

Every time I could, I called her, and when that wasn't possible, I took time to write. I missed her a great deal, and sometimes just hearing her voice on the other end of the telephone helped. But as soon as I heard her say "Hello," I lost all awareness of time—and by the end of the first month, our telephone bill totaled three hundred dollars!

We had planned to be married on New Year's Eve. Our thought was to start off the new year together. But as we watched the phone bills mount up month after month, we determined that it would be much more practical to get married sooner.

As I mentioned before, Ronnie was engaged to Marilyn, Pat's best friend. They faced similar circumstances during their engagement, including the long-distance telephone bills.

Finally, through a number of different circumstances, the four of us decided to have a double wedding. Ronnie and I were very close as brothers, and we also ministered together on a full-time basis. Pat and Marilyn were best friends, so it seemed like a natural. We compromised on the date and chose October 21!

There was only one problem. Ronnie and I owned a Pontiac 2 Plus 2 (a glorified GTO). We shared a lot, but we didn't plan to have a double honeymoon too. With one car between us, we weren't quite sure what to do.

Just a few weeks before the wedding, Ronnie and I were holding special meetings in Baxley, Georgia. This was to be one of our last engagements before the double wedding. We had scheduled no meetings the week prior to the wedding or the week after the wedding. Ronnie and I were eager to get back home and spend some time with Marilyn and Pat before the wedding and help with any last-minute details. Up to this time, I had only spent that week in Memphis with Pat. The remainder of our courtship had been by telephone and by mail.

As we were closing our meetings in Baxley, Georgia, a gentleman offered to loan me a car for our honeymoon. It was a canary yellow Chevrolet convertible! I knew that this was God's provision for us, for we had no other access to an automobile. Once again I saw God's hand of blessing supply our needs.

Following the wedding and the reception, Ronnie and his wife drove off in the Pontiac 2 Plus 2, and Pat and I drove off in the borrowed yellow convertible. As Ronnie and I waved good-bye to each other, we knew that life would be different from now on. And what a wonderful change it would be. For as we traveled from church to church, we would no longer have to go alone. From now on, Pat and Marilyn would be coming along.

## HERE AND NOW

Pat and I were in our late teens then, and at the writing of this book, we have celebrated thirty years of marriage. Those years have taken us through many different stages of life. We have encountered numerous opportunities and challenges along the way, and with the Lord Jesus at the center of our marriage and home, we have celebrated the victories together and overcome the trials as we trusted God together for the answer.

The victories have been easily enjoyed together, and throughout our marriage we have had many opportunities to celebrate some wonderful times. But when trials and tragedies come, they are much more difficult to deal with. Obviously our greatest challenge in this area was when David was snatched from our lives. I can say without hesitation that experience was the most difficult for us to handle, individually and as a husband and wife. I'm told that many couples who lose a child in such a tragic way often fail to recover and a great percentage of these marriages eventually end in divorce.

It is no understatement to say that we faced many difficult days. But the underlying element that has sustained our relationship is commitment—commitment to the Lord Jesus and to one another.

In the life of the believer, life is really a series of commitments. For Pat and me, our commitments began with the first and most important: when we committed our lives to Jesus Christ and trusted Him for our salvation. Pat was only five years old when she invited Jesus Christ to be the Lord of her life; I was thirteen years of age when I made the same commitment.

As teenagers we sensed God's call upon our lives and felt strongly that we were set apart for His service. I began preaching the gospel at the age of about fifteen. As an eighteen-year-old, I began to travel with my brother, Ronnie, in an evangelistic ministry similar to our father's.

Then on October 21, 1966, Pat and I made a commitment to one another in marriage before God. We promised to love each other until death separated us, and we regarded that as a very sacred commitment before God. We also committed our lives to serve the Lord together in ministry, taking the good news of the gospel to "whosoever will." And as Pat says, the commitments we made in the good times were sacred enough to carry us through the troubled times. There was never any doubt about how sure our commitment was in the good times. Only in the face of a trial and only as the winds of life blow against you do you know how sure your foundation is. Only then do you understand how firm your commitment is.

## COMMITMENTS TO BUILD UPON

Commitments in the life of the believer are sometimes like the pilings that are driven into the bedrock to create a strong foundation for whatever is to be built upon it. The foundations of some of the greatest superstructures in the world today are driven several stories deep into the earth. Yet, because the foundation is below ground level, only the lofty engineering feat of concrete, steel, and glass that stands upon that foundation captures man's attention and praise. The carefully placed pilings and foundational materials are never noted on the skyline of a city.

A perfect example of this, in my opinion, is the Gateway Arch in St. Louis, Missouri. A landmark 650 feet high, it is one of the most prominent engineering feats of the century. When the winds blow, the Arch can potentially sway more than a foot. Although that is somewhat frightening to consider, it is imperative to remember that such superstructures are built to withstand extremes like this. The constant changes in the wind, weather, and movement of the earth must be calculated, and considerations must be made in the construction for such changes.

Buildings of this nature depend largely upon two components for their survival: the foundation and expansion joints. First, there must be a strong foundation. Huge pilings are rammed down to the bedrock level in the earth, far below ground level. Tons of concrete and steel are deposited around these pilings after they are in place, filling every cavity. This is absolutely critical to the construction, even though it will never be seen once the structure is completed. All the fancy ornaments and embellishments above ground can never compensate for a poor foundation. No matter how masterfully a building is finished, there are no shortcuts for a strong and sure foundation.

It is interesting to note the comments of Jesus regarding a house that was built by a reputable contractor. "The rain descended, the floods came, and the winds blew and beat on that house; and it did not fall, for it was founded on the rock" (Matthew 7:25). How significant that the building mentioned was not situated in ideal conditions, but its foundation kept it from falling.

Jesus Christ is that Rock upon which we stand. The foundation of our lives must be sure, established upon the eternal Son of God, Jesus Christ. For Pat, this foundation began to be established at the young age of five.

In addition to a strong and firm foundation, a building must also have flexibility. This is achieved by including expansion joints in the plans of the building. Expansion joints are built in to allow a minute degree of movement at every level. Without this tolerance, the structure could splinter and fall under the stress.

The apostle Paul submitted this affirmation that the grace of God can miraculously put expansion joints into the lives of men and enable them to stand when he said, "Who shall separate us from the love of Christ? Shall tribulation, or distress, or persecution, or famine, or nakedness, or peril, or sword? ... Yet in all these things we are more than conquerors through Him who loved us" (Romans 8:35, 37).

In his testimony to Timothy, Paul declared, "I know whom I have believed and am persuaded that He is able to keep what I have committed to Him" (2 Timothy 1:12).

Our commitments bring the foundation and flexibility that we need at various times in our lives. If I were to step back and examine the commitments that my wife has made through the years, I believe that it would be very easy to see how the strength of one commitment has led to the next one in her life.

She first committed her life to the Lord and that commitment extends to eternity. Much like the strength that a foundation brings to a superstructure, so that ultimate commitment provides a foundation upon which to build a life with the Lord and with your fellow man.

Next, she has made a commitment as my wife in marriage. That commitment is one that will continue until death separates us.

Her third and very important commitment is as a mother. That commitment is to the family and extends not only to this generation but also to future generations. I will discuss this commitment at length in the next chapter, for it is expressed in many different ways.

As I mentioned before, Pat says the commitments we made in the good times were sacred enough to carry us through the troubled times. In looking back over the past thirty years, I can see how true this is, for we could never have anticipated the degree of troubled times or the number of difficult days that we would face together. But with God's help, and because of our commitment to Him and to one another, we have walked, hand in hand, through some of the darkest days of our lives. The journey through that darkness seemed endless at times, but through prayer and with the Lord's help, the darkness did begin to vanish. As we emerged from that darkness, we discovered a beauty and bright hope for tomorrow that lie just beyond today.

## CHAPTER 10

# COMMITMENTS: BUILDING BLOCKS FOR TOMORROW

S ince the first time her beautiful brown eyes captured my heart, I have seen something in Pat that I have always admired—commitment. This trait—the ability to pursue and accomplish what she deems most important—is one of her greatest strengths. It is one of the things I love most about her.

From that first Thursday evening when we attended the Church of God national convention meeting together, strong commitment was very evident in Pat's life. Her devotion and commitment to God were apparent. They were a part of who she was. At the time, I didn't realize how much this quality in Pat would affect our life together, or what wealth it would bring to our relationship and, later, to our family.

Sometime after our initial meeting that Thursday, I discovered that she had committed her life to Jesus Christ in a vacation Bible school (summer daytime program at her church, similar to Sunday school) when she was just a little girl.

Although Pat was only five years old at the time, she says she remembers responding from her front-row seat as the invitation was given. She recalls walking forward and kneeling at a well-worn, wine-colored, velvet pulpit chair. As she poured out her heart to God in prayer that day, tears ran down her face and joy filled her heart as she invited Jesus Christ to be her Lord and Savior.

Pat fondly reflects on this time in her life because it still affects her today. She won a prize at that vacation Bible school, a wooden plaque that said,

> Only one life, will soon be past.
> Only what's done for Christ will last.

She is reminded of this each morning as she prepares for the day because that cherished wooden plaque hangs near her closet in our home. The plaque is old, some of the corners are knocked off, and it really doesn't fit into most decors today. But regardless of the appearance, the statement displayed on the old plaque has always fit into Pat's life. Each morning it greets her, reminding her of a commitment she made many years ago.

## HOME IS WHERE THE HEART IS

I've already shared with you how we met and got married. Not long after we were married, I began to understand commitment in a new and different way. From the moment we said "I do," Pat's commitment to me as my wife was evident.

That first year of our marriage, Pat and I, along with Ronnie and his wife, traveled from city to city and church to church. Sometimes we were on the road sixteen weeks at a time before returning home briefly.

Our itinerary was quite busy, but the honorariums we received had to support two households now. Consequently, our accommodations on the road were not always "deluxe."

Pat and I stayed in just one room, and that was our temporary "home" for the duration of our meetings in that town. Even though we didn't stay in a palace, Pat made me feel like a king! I was always amazed at her extraordinary ability to make that single, little room so homey and such a sanctuary from the world.

To make the hotel room more homelike, sometimes Pat would rearrange the furniture and move things around. She would have everything organized, including my clothing. She would hang my suits a certain way in the closet, arranging my shirts and ties in an orderly manner so that everything that coordinated with a particular suit hung together with that suit. She gave the same care and attention to my shoes, always making certain that they were ready. From the very beginning, Pat was meticulous like this. Her attention to being so organized made the traveling much easier and gave us more time to spend together.

I realize that this was an expression of her commitment to me because it truly demonstrated her love for me as well as support for the dreams and goals I had in life.

When the boys came along, Pat's commitment to our family was only strengthened. Being a wife and a mother is definitely a full-time commitment, and this was a commitment that Pat joyfully accepted. No matter where we were or what we were doing, we enjoyed ourselves. Pat made do with what we had, improvising when necessary.

Wherever we went and whatever we did, Pat's positive outlook, combined with her love and commitment for me and the boys, made us strong as husband and wife and also as a family unit. That commitment has played a major role in bringing us to where we are today. And I know that it is also a building block for the future.

## WORDS OF WISDOM

The following words are taken from some notes that Pat jotted down recently about husbands and wives. I want to share them with you, for I feel that they contain great wisdom.

"As a wife, get to know your husband. Listen to his words and his heart. Find out what his dreams are, and support his aspirations. Learn when to speak and when to listen. Learning about his fears will also tell you a great deal about him and will help you understand him better."

I can tell you from personal experience that this is exactly what Pat has done throughout our marriage. Although her words were directed toward women, I think this advice is appropriate for men as well.

For us, these principles were put to their greatest test when David was snatched away by death's cold grasp. In the midst of all that pain and sorrow, Pat was there for me and for Tony.

I felt almost as if I had been paralyzed by the grief. This temporary emotional paralysis left me weak and unable to recognize what Pat was going through. I was more inclined to express what I was feeling, while Pat was more quiet. At the time I thought this was how Pat had chosen to deal with her grief. I didn't realize until years later, however, that Pat's silence was for my benefit and not hers. She saw me suffering and chose to withdraw and internalize her pain in an attempt to spare me any additional grief just because she loved me and didn't want to add to my sorrow. She responded similarly to Tony. She did a lot of thinking and tried to figure out everything in her mind, failing to realize that she had not been talking about her feelings. She maintained that as a wife and mother, she could not allow herself to be selfish in her grief, and she allowed Tony and me to grieve in our own ways.

The book *Lament for a Son* addresses Pat's suffering:

> Suffering is the shout of "No" by one's whole existence to that over which one suffers—the shout of "No" by nerves and gut and gland and heart to pain, to death, to injustice, to depression, to hunger, to humiliation, to bondage, to abandonment. And sometimes, when the cry is intense, there emerges a radiance which elsewhere seldom appears: a glow of courage, of love, of insight, of selflessness, of faith. In that radiance we see best what humanity was meant to be.[1]

## BACK TO NORMAL

"Normal" as it existed before a tragedy never returns, just as grief never really goes away. It just becomes part of us as we learn to deal with it, finding moments of happiness in the memories we have of the deceased loved one.

When a flower is plucked from the ground, it takes time for the ground to be repaired. When a loved one is taken from us, the shock is so great that it takes time for the healing.

The day I discovered that I could keep my wonderful memories of David and give God the pain, grief's hold on me began to lessen. Even though "normal" as I knew it was gone forever, I knew I had to go on, for Pat's sake and for Tony's. Life was moving on—with or without me—and I had to make a decision about whether or not I was going to be part of it.

## CHAPTER 11

# A MOTHER'S PRAYERS

I love you, Tony," Pat said as she gave Tony a big hug, followed by a big kiss on the cheek.

"I love you, too, Mom," Tony responded.

"What about me, Mom?" David said in his jovial way as he came bounding up behind Pat.

Pat turned around and threw her arms around David as she planted a big kiss on his face. "I love you, David," she said as she tousled his curly, black hair. "You're both very special to me."

This was the norm in our home from the time Tony and David were born. Pat always hugged the boys and reminded them of her love for them. They were never too old for a bedtime hug and a kiss, followed by "I love you."

Pat's commitment as a mother has always been strong. Since the first moment she held Tony in her arms as a newborn, she has been strongly committed to being a good mother. She always showered him with love and affection and made him feel so special. When David came along just seventeen months later, he enjoyed the same loving care and attention.

In my opinion, Pat has always been a wonderful mother because she has given herself to it 100 percent. That is her personality. No matter what she has ever done, whether it was sports or her job or relationships with those whom she loved, she has given 100 percent.

For Pat, being a mother was much more than making sure that the children were fed, clothed, and sheltered. It was more than kissing a "boo-boo" on a scuffed knee and placing a bandage on the area to protect it. Being a mother was more than simply making the boys feel special, although she always did that with perfection.

You see, all of these things I mentioned represent the natural aspects of being a good mother, and for Pat, this is only part of what she views as her responsibility as a mother. She feels that she has a responsibility in the spiritual realm that extends beyond the physical or natural, and she faithfully has given attention to that area as well.

One aspect of the realm beyond the natural in which Pat invested many hours was in the training of our children in the ways of the Lord. The Bible says, "Train up a child in the way he should go, / And when he is old he will not depart from it" (Proverbs 22:6).

Godly parents had laid a strong foundation in Pat's life, and her family was very important to her because she was an only child. As she became an adult and eventually a mother, she chose to follow the example her parents had set for her because of the impact they had upon her life. Her earliest memories include times when her parents read stories to her from the Bible and taught her eternal principles. As a young child of only five years of age, she knelt and invited Jesus Christ to be her Lord and Savior. Through example and experience she learned to take her needs and concerns to the Lord in prayer, and when she did, God answered her prayers.

## PRAY, DADDY!

When discussing the topic of prayer, Pat often reflects on a time when she was only nine years old. She was very ill, so her mother placed a thermometer in her mouth to determine how severe her condition was. Almost immediately the thermometer exploded in her mouth due to the high fever. In the natural realm, a parent might rush a child to the doctor under these circumstances because it is understood that the mercury contained in a thermometer is poisonous. But rather than rushing Pat to the doctor, she recalls her father's response: prayer. He immediately fell to his knees and prayed for Pat. Rather than rushing her to the doctor, Pat says her father rushed her to the throne room of heaven and interceded before God Almighty on her behalf. God intervened miraculously, and in a matter of moments her fever was gone, there were no ill effects of the mercury, and she was asking for something to eat!

## PAT'S COMMITMENT TO PRAYER

Pat's childhood experiences, along with her rich spiritual heritage, have taught her the importance of prayer. As a result, she has established every area of her life on that foundation, and it has made a world of difference in our family. In fact, I don't know where we would be today without her steadfast commitment to prayer.

First, she has committed herself to prayer for me as her husband and as the head of our home. She has upheld me in prayer as a minister of the gospel and supported me in my aspirations. Because of the prayers she has prayed in private, great results have occurred publicly. My "success" has been acknowledged and applauded by men while heaven has recorded and answered the prayers Pat prayed in secret.

She has faithfully upheld our marriage in prayer, and I know that her prayers have sustained us on many occasions. Her prayers have undergirded us and helped to carry us through uncharted waters where other couples have succumbed to the raging seas of sorrow and despair.

As a mother she has upheld our children in prayer and trusted the Lord for His wisdom and help in training them in His ways. In Psalm 127:3 we see that "Children are a gift of the LORD"

(NASB). In Hebrew, *gift* means "property, a possession." Truly, God has loaned us His property, or possessions, to care for and to enjoy for a certain period of time. Pat has always believed that because our children are from the Lord, we as Christian parents have a responsibility to pray for them. She always prayed faithfully for Tony and David and trusted God to lead her as she helped to mold their lives for the Lord.

## A TALK WITH MOM

I can recall a time when the boys were getting to be teenagers and began to be faced with peer pressure in the area of drinking. Pat sat the boys down and had a talk with them about alcohol. Because she had witnessed the devastating results of alcohol on some of her family members, she never liked anything that was remotely connected to alcohol. In addition, some members of my own family, including my brother and an uncle, had also experienced problems at times with alcohol.

That day as she talked to the boys, she explained some of the problems various relatives had encountered with alcohol. She told them that they didn't stand "a ghost of a chance" against alcohol because of the family history on both sides. She cautioned them about how addictive alcohol could be and reminded them how it had affected many people who were close to us.

At the time Pat didn't realize what she was saying, for in the years that followed the effects of alcohol would impact her own life in a very traumatic way—when David was killed. And even in the darkness of sorrow that surrounded her during those days, her prayers carried her through when there seemed to be nowhere to turn. Because she was an only child and essentially had no one to talk to as a child, she grew up solving her own problems. This approach became so natural to her that when David was taken from us, she responded in the same way.

Everything she had ever faced in life up to that time she had faced alone. This forced her to work everything out on her own as well. When she saw how Tony and I were hurting, she tried to spare us by keeping her feelings and emotions to herself. She internalized her pain and put off dealing with her own feelings initially because she didn't know what to do.

Because it is impossible to deal with everything at once, I realize now that Pat attempted to suppress her anger and the nagging questions that I faced. She merely succeeded in dealing with the tragedy of David's death on the surface. Because Pat was quieter about her grief, many people mistakenly thought that she was dealing with our loss better than I was. However, the truth of the matter is that Pat was really just suffering in silence. Only as she learned to cast her own cares of grief and pain upon the Lord in prayer did she begin to experience victory and find hope.

## COMMITMENTS THAT STAND IN THE MIDST OF CHANGE

Many things changed in our home after David was snatched away in death. Up to that time, Pat had been traveling with me from time to time, praying for me, and working side by side with me in our evangelistic ministry.

Following David's death, Pat made a decision to stay home for Tony's sake. Although Tony was almost eighteen years old, Pat recommitted herself to the home life. She didn't stay at home because of a fear of what Tony would do, because she had committed him to the Lord years before. In prayer the Lord directed her to keep our home stable. She was committed to the family, and as a result she obeyed God's command for her life at that time.

Although much changed in our home in the weeks and months following David's death, one thing that remained constant was Pat's commitment to prayer, for which I am so grateful. Pat often said, "I can't change what has happened, but I can pray that the best will come out of this." And that is what ultimately happened when Pat prepared to say good night to Tony with a hug, a kiss, and an "I love you, Tony."

One night when Tony came home from a night out with his friends from church, Pat approached him to say the usual good night. As she hugged him, she was stunned! She couldn't believe it, but she was certain that she smelled alcohol on Tony's breath.

A torrent of emotions swept over her. Instantly she felt as though she was a total failure as a mother. She asked herself, *Don't I relate to him? Have his peers influenced him more than Steve and I? How could Tony turn to alcohol when that very thing was what stole David from our family?*

Pat said nothing to me about the incident at the time, but in the heat of the conflict that raged within, Pat's commitment to prayer rose up within her. And as it did, the real enemy was unmasked and the questions vanished. When reflecting on that time, Pat still speaks with such feeling and conviction. She recalls standing in the den of our home and taking her stand against the real enemy—the devil. As she fell to her knees, she said, "Satan, you took one of my sons through alcohol. You will not take another. This son will not live the life of an alcoholic. Your influence will be defeated in Tony's life, and I will pray until victory comes!"

Her commitment to prayer for her son became her focus. She was relentless as she petitioned God on Tony's behalf. In fact, she was so determined to gain the victory through prayer that for the next three months she ate only one meal each day. She chose to abstain from food during the other two mealtimes to give herself to prayer for Tony.

And prayer brought the victory! In Chapter 8 you read the wonderful account of how Tony's life was transformed. I know beyond a shadow of a doubt that Tony's transformation came about as a direct result of Pat's commitment to prayer. During those months of prayer, Pat said nothing to me about Tony's problems. She went straight to the throne room of heaven, just as her father had done when the thermometer exploded in her mouth when she was a child. As Scripture says, "The effective, fervent prayer of a righteous man [or woman] avails much" (James 5:16).

Pat's prayers produced results in Tony's life. And through this situation, Pat was reminded once again that when bad things happen, prayer is the answer.

## WHEN BAD THINGS HAPPEN

If there ever was a man who loved and obeyed God, it was Job. Yet he experienced a great deal of pain, loss, and tragedy.

Today all we have to do is pick up a newspaper in any part of the world and we can read of tragedy touching the just and the unjust. Tragedy is no respecter of persons. Bad things happen to good people.

Bad things can come in the form of sickness, misfortune, disaster, or anything else that may be deemed "bad," but, nevertheless, good people are not necessarily exempt from bad things. Pastor Benny Hinn recently shared a wonderful example of this fact through the life of Peter's mother-in-law. In sharing the story, he also showed how vital prayer was in bringing a resolution to the problem.

In Luke 4:38 and 39 we read: "Now He arose from the synagogue and entered Simon's house. But Simon's wife's mother was sick with a high fever, and they made request of Him concerning her. So He stood over her and rebuked the fever, and it left her. And immediately she arose and served them." Peter's mother-in-law was taken with a high fever. Today a fever is not often considered life-threatening because of the wonderful breakthroughs in medicine that have made miracle drugs like Tylenol, Advil, aspirin, and other pain relievers standard fare in most American households. But for Peter's mother-in-law, a high fever could very well have been life-threatening. Peter was so concerned about her well-being that he asked Jesus to come and heal her.

## TAKE IT TO JESUS

This is the day of peptic ulcers, headaches, and tension. It is a time of frustration, worry, and anxiety. It's a period of distress, confusion, and almost unbearable burdens. As times become more complex and mankind drifts farther away from the simple life of Jesus Christ, difficulties and troubles will become correspondingly more complex.

Everywhere humans are seeking a solution for their problems. By the thousands they are consulting specialists who have problems of their own that they cannot solve. Many of these specialists are trying to solve the problems of humanity with the godless theories of atheists and infidels, but the clients often leave their offices more disturbed than when they went in. A number of them do a good job of diagnosing their clients' difficulties, but in reality they have little or no solution for their ills. This is simply because they do not realize that Jesus Christ is the solution to human problems and to every human need.

The Word of God says in Philippians 4:19, "And my God shall supply all your need according to His riches in glory by Christ Jesus." I often sing with Benny Hinn in his Miracle Crusades a song titled "All in the Name of Jesus." The lyrics say

*All that I longed for and all that I need,*
*It's all in the name of Jesus.*

Jesus has everything you and I need. It seems so simple to say that Jesus Christ is the answer when facing the complex problems of life or frustrations. But Jesus said, "Come to Me, all you who labor and are heavy laden, and I will give you rest" (Matthew 11:28).

In Scripture Jesus never turned anyone away who came to Him with cares, burdens, problems, sickness, or sin. There was no problem that He could not master. And He has not changed for He is "the same yesterday, today, and forever" (Hebrews 13:8).

The hearts of men and women are failing them for fear. Multitudes are on the verge of nervous breakdowns and mental disorders. Worry is robbing humankind of its health. This generation is harassed by fear and anxiety. Millions of dollars are spent each year to erase the lines and wrinkles that worry and anxiety have slowly but surely etched upon our faces.

God's Word tells us we don't have to bear our burdens alone. We are invited to cast our cares upon the Lord in 1 Peter 5:7, where we read, "Cast all your anxiety on him because he cares for you" (NIV). In other words, unload your distresses and leave them with the Lord.

"What a Friend We Have in Jesus" is a well-known hymn, considered by many to be a classic. Although it is sung in many churches, we often fail to apply the familiar lyrics, which say,

> *What a friend we have in Jesus,*
> *All our sins and griefs to bear!*
> *What a privilege to carry*
> *Everything to God in prayer!*
> *O what peace we often forfeit,*
> *O what needless pain we bear.*
> *All because we do not carry*
> *Everything to God in prayer.*
>
> *Have we trials and temptations?*
> *Is there trouble anywhere?*
> *We should never be discouraged—*
> *Take it to the Lord in prayer!*
> *Can we find a friend so faithful,*
> *Who will all our sorrows share?*
> *Jesus knows our every weakness—*
> *Take it to the Lord in prayer!*

Joseph Scriven wrote these beautiful lyrics in the mid-1800s. He had wealth, education, a devoted family, and a pleasant life in his native Ireland. Then unexpected tragedy entered his life. On the night before Scriven's scheduled wedding, his fiancée drowned. In his deep sorrow, Joseph realized that he could find the solace and support he needed only in his dearest friend, Jesus.

Some time later when his mother became ill, he wrote a

comforting letter to her, enclosing the words of his newly written poem with the prayer that these brief lines would remind her of a never-failing heavenly Friend.[1]

Like the writer of this great hymn, we also can find relief from our burdens and cares when we turn to the Lord Jesus Christ, "a friend that sticks closer than a brother."

I once read a little poem that I think illustrates so well the love and care our heavenly Father has for us.

*Said the robin to the sparrow, "I should really like to know*
*Why these anxious human beings rush about and worry so."*
*Said the sparrow to the robin, "Friend, I think that it must be,*
*That they have no Heavenly Father, such as cares for you and me."*

Matthew 6:26 says, "Look at the birds! They don't worry about what to eat—they don't need to sow or reap or store up food—for your heavenly Father feeds them. And you are far more valuable to him than they are" (TLB). Your heavenly Father is concerned about the things that concern you. There is no problem too great or too small for Him. When you cast your cares upon Him in prayer, He will turn your heartaches into hallelujahs, your burdens into blessings, and your troubles into triumphs.

I have often heard Pastor Benny Hinn quote Isaiah 54:17, "No weapon formed against you shall prosper." That doesn't mean that no weapon will be formed against you. But if you pray, any weapon or opposition that is formed against you will not prosper.

What was meant as a weapon against Pat and me for our demise was destroyed through the power of prayer. If you are facing some form of opposition, take it to the Lord in prayer, and pray until the answer comes!

## CHAPTER 12

# LEARNING TO PRAY

Wouldn't this life be wonderful if you could somehow guarantee that you and your loved ones would never face any kind of trouble in life? Problem-free insurance that lasts a lifetime? What a fabulous concept!

Unfortunately, there is no such thing!

But the child of God has a much more powerful affiliate available than any insurance company, for through prayer a believer can access heaven's throne room and petition the Creator of heaven and earth, God Almighty, for help.

## WHAT TO DO WHEN TROUBLE COMES YOUR WAY

Some individuals mistakenly think that when a person is a Christian, life will be trouble free—no problems, no sorrow, no misfortune, no heartaches. To become born again and experience the glorious transformation of having your sins washed away through the shed blood of Jesus Christ when you repent and ask Him to cleanse your heart from sin is the greatest miracle that can happen to any individual. The peace that comes when a man or woman begins to live in a right relationship with Jesus Christ is beyond description, for it will one day carry him or her to an eternal dwelling place with God. One of the great benefits of being a Christian is the incredible hope that extends beyond the grave into the glory of God's tomorrow. However, the life of the believer carries no guarantee for any insulation from trouble or problems here and now.

Jesus said, "These things I have spoken to you, that in Me you might have peace. In the world you will have tribulation; but be of good cheer, I have overcome the world" (John 16:33).

Our peace and our security rest in Jesus Christ and in His overcoming power. When He said, "Be of good cheer," He was really telling us not to worry, because He has overcome the world. He has gained the victory over sin and death, and now nothing can separate us from Him or the love of God.

## THE SCRIPTURAL PERSPECTIVE ON TROUBLE

The Bible provides some wonderful insights on what to do when trouble comes our way. Included within its sacred pages we find examples of what to do and what not to do when dealing with trouble. We can learn some very important lessons from both perspectives.

The story of King Hezekiah in 2 Kings 18–20 illustrates clearly one of the best options we as believers have available to us when trouble comes our way, because the Bible declares that Hezekiah faced some perilous times as king.

He became king of Judah after the death of his father, Ahaz, a king who did not keep the commandments of the Lord. When Ahaz died, Hezekiah became king and immediately began to put right the wrong that Ahaz had done as king. He repaired the temple and ordered that the sacrifices and services formerly held in the temple begin again. He also commanded that they be conducted just as the law of the Lord said they should be carried out.

At this time Sennacherib was the king of Assyria. Hezekiah was king of Judah, but at the time Judah as a nation, along with Israel and Syria, was in the hands of Assyria. This made the kings of these three nations subject to the Assyrian king, who imposed heavy taxes on them annually.

In the fourteenth year of King Hezekiah's reign, he decided that it was time for Judah to be free again, so he refused to pay the taxes. He strengthened the walls of Jerusalem and prepared to defend the country against any attack the Assyrians might render.

The Assyrian army attacked from the west, and soon some of the western cities were under the control of Assyria. When King Hezekiah realized that his army was not strong enough to effectively defend Judah, he sent messengers to Sennacherib, king of Assyria, asking for peace. He also changed his previously held position regarding payment of taxes. He tried to affirm his desire for peace by promising to pay whatever taxes were demanded.

When an agreement was finally reached, the total of the tax due was so staggering that Judah did not have the necessary funds to cover it. Therefore, Hezekiah was forced to have gold removed from several areas of the temple. This included the gold that had been applied to the refurbished temple doors, along with other gold that had been used inside in the restoration of the temple.

After all this wealth had been transferred to Sennacherib to pay the high taxes, he still was not satisfied. Sennacherib's hunger for power and control drove him on, and by the time the taxes were paid, he had already attacked the lower Judean cities surrounding Jerusalem. Then he thought, "Why not send an army to attack Jerusalem and conquer it as well?"

He sent three of his princes ahead of the army to deliver a taunting, blasphemous letter to King Hezekiah. In this letter he belittled the king, his army, and his God. He bragged about how great he was as king and how mighty his army was. He even boasted about how big his god was.

This posed a problem of major proportions. How was Hezekiah going to respond? How was he going to react?

Remember, trouble is not what gets you into trouble. Trouble is not what separates you from God. The determining factor is how you respond and react to trouble. It can either bring you closer to God or push you farther away.

Before we look at what King Hezekiah did, let's consider what he did not do.

First, he did not ignore the problem and simply expect it to go away. Remember, denying a problem won't make it go away. You have to face your trouble. Do something about it. If you run from it, it will run after you. Every time you run from your trouble, that problem will follow right behind you.

Second, he didn't respond with counterthreats. He didn't react to Sennacherib's prideful boasting in like manner and say, "Excuse me, but don't you know who *I* am! *I* am King Hezekiah." There is only one way in which you should ever use the pronoun "I" in times of trouble:

> *I can do all things through Christ who strengthens me."*
> (Philippians 4:13)

Don't ever try to use the pronoun "I" to refer to yourself and your ability by saying, "*I* can do this." No, *you* can't. Let God do it.

## WHO'S DOING THE DRIVING?

When my boys were young, I would often allow them to sit on my lap and pretend that they were driving the car as we rode down the highway. They loved to take turns and help me drive. They would put their hands on the steering wheel just as they always saw me do, thinking, of course, that they were operating the automobile. But what they often failed to notice was that I, too, had my hands on the wheel, carefully guiding the car to its final destination.

In many ways, our lives are like that. I may have my hands on the steering wheel of my life, but because I am His child, God is directing the course of my life, helping me arrive at my destination safely. I'm not in control; He is.

The Bible says, "Trust in the LORD with all your heart, And lean not on your own understanding" (Proverbs 3:5). Don't try to figure it out; put your life in God's hands and "He shall direct your paths"(v.6).

King Hezekiah did not appeal for sympathy from those rulers who were around him. In times of trouble, the thing that you and I need the least is sympathy, for sympathy does not help. In my darkest hours following David's death, many kind and wonderful individuals expressed their sympathy to Pat and me. Their words of comfort and love helped get us through those long, lonely days. But the impact of their words was short-lived.

When the funeral was over, their concern and frequent visits soon faded into nothingness. It was at that time that the real struggle actually began. When I was all alone in the heat of the battle and the enemy of my soul was harassing me, the kind words of comfort faded quickly from my memory. All the words of sympathy and loving concern did not equip me for battle, but God's Word did. It was in those moments that God's Word brought reassurance and strengthened me as I prayed and meditated upon familiar Scriptures like these:

*He who is in you is greater than he who is in the world.*
(1 John 4:4).

*Yea, though I walk through the valley of the shadow of death,*
*I will fear no evil;*
*For You are with me.* (Psalm 23:4)

*Cast your burden on the LORD,*
*And He shall sustain you;*
*He shall never permit the righteous to be moved.* (Psalm 55:22)

In the natural realm, caring people try to do their best. But that, my friend, is all they can offer. God will never just "do the best He can" for you. He will do exceedingly, abundantly beyond anything you can ask or think if you will just call upon Him. He will lift you out of the valley and carry you up to a mountaintop. He will build bridges over your troubled waters. You will be victorious and free when God is in your life.

## HEZEKIAH'S SECRET WEAPON

Hezekiah had a secret weapon that he used when faced with Sennacherib's challenge. What did he do?

"And Hezekiah received the letter from the hand of the messengers, and read it; and Hezekiah went up to the house of the LORD, and spread it before the LORD. Then Hezekiah prayed to the LORD" (Isaiah 37:14–15).

At a time of extreme adversity, Hezekiah prayed. He knew that he had no adequate military defense systems to prevail against an adversary like Sennacherib. But he knew that through prayer he could deploy all the armies of the hosts of heaven and his enemy would be crushed and defeated.

Isaiah 37:36–38 give us an account of what happened. The angel of the Lord visited the camp of the Assyrians during the night, and before morning 185,000 of the soldiers were dead. When King Sennacherib arrived and discovered what had happened, he took the remaining soldiers and returned to Nineveh in his own country. Some time after he returned, his own sons killed him with a sword while he was worshiping before an idol.

## FOUR STEPS TO VICTORY

Hezekiah did four things to destroy the enemy. You and I can see every enemy in our lives destroyed if we will follow his example.

The first thing he did was go to the house of the Lord. He had a relationship with the Lord and knew where he could find the Lord when he faced trouble.

The second thing that he did was pray. He didn't hesitate but turned to prayer immediately as the only answer. He didn't call his friends or other people first before going to God. He also didn't check with anyone. He went directly to God and began to pray immediately.

The third thing that he did was to give the problem to the Lord. As he spread that harassing letter from Sennacherib before the altar of the Lord, he asked God to come to the aid of His people in their hour of need. He didn't try to impress God with eloquent prayers. He simply presented his need to the Lord and waited for God to intervene.

Today, just as in Hezekiah's day, God is looking for those who will seek Him with all of their hearts. It doesn't matter where you live or who you know, what you do or how much money you have. If you want, you can take all day long to tell God about your great accomplishments and who you think you are, but He is not easily impressed. There is only one thing that moves God, and that is faith. You touch God through your faith.

If you are facing what appears to be an insurmountable mountain, remember, faith moves God and God moves mountains. Go to God in faith, and trust Him for the answer.

The fourth thing that King Hezekiah did was pray until he prayed through. This was a great key to his victory and can be the key to your much needed victory as well.

King Hezekiah waited to hear from God. He sent two men to the prophet Isaiah to inquire if there was any message from God regarding the situation he was facing. The word they brought back was, "The Lord says, 'Do not be afraid of what the Assyrians have said. The king of Assyria will not enter this city nor will he even shoot an arrow or attack it in any way. He will return to his own land the same way he came and will be killed by the sword in his own land.'" Hezekiah did not give up until he heard from God, and God rescued him just as He promised.

This is a powerful key to remember: when you are facing trouble or disaster, pray until you pray through. James 5:16 states, "The effective, fervent prayer of a righteous man [or woman] avails much." In other words, prayer works! Prayer brings things to pass that would not come to pass otherwise.

I have faced troublesome times and turmoil on many different occasions during my lifetime, but one time in particular stands out in my mind. In that time of distress I turned to God in prayer, for there was no one else to turn to; no one else could help. But before I share this story, I want to set the stage to help you understand the background of the situation.

As I mentioned earlier, I lost my father when I was very young. He was an evangelist, and I'm told that he held great healing meetings and preached with power. As an evangelist he traveled a great deal, coming and going all the time.

Because my brother and I were very little, my mother had grown accustomed to seeing him drive off to his next meeting while she stayed home with Ronnie, my sister, Judy, and me. But one day he left for his last trip.

He had packed his things and was getting ready to leave to go preach. Following his normal good-bye ritual, he kissed and hugged each of us, grabbed his suitcase, walked out the door, and drove away. I can remember how my mother often stood at the door, watching until his car vanished from sight.

As I grew older, she sometimes reminisced about that day as she watched him drive away for the last time. He left in the usual manner with the good-byes and hugs, and mother stood at the door as usual and watched his car melt into the horizon. But he never came back as usual because he died while preaching at that meeting.

Because my father died and did not return, my mother became reluctant to have Ronnie and me gone from the house as we became teenagers. Her hesitation affected everything that happened outside the four walls of our house, including holding a job. Being the oldest, however, Ronnie finally convinced mother to let him get a job. He began working at a restaurant named Roy's Little Garden. It wasn't the greatest job, but it was a job, nonetheless. The hours were fairly predictable, so mother learned to accept it.

On one occasion, however, Ronnie's boss decided to have a staff meeting after work. As an employee, it was mandatory for Ronnie to stay for the meeting. Ronnie had no way to contact my mother and me regarding his delay in coming home. The staff meeting turned out to be very lengthy, lasting until three o'clock in the morning! Needless to say, my mother was at home, weeping and praying. Fear and worry tormented her throughout the long night hours as she wrestled with the unknown. Her husband had been taken in death unexpectedly; what had become of her son? He had been due home hours before—what had happened to him?

I was about thirteen years old at the time, and I can remember how terrible the agony was that tormented my mother. It was late, and I was getting worried too. I felt so helpless. I didn't want my mother to worry so. Finally, not knowing what else to do, I turned to God in prayer just as Hezekiah did. I quietly went to the next room and prayed, "Lord, You've got to help me. I'm worried about Ronnie, and Mother is terrified. Please protect him and bring him home."

Almost immediately, that still, small voice that I had come to know whispered these words of assurance to my heart: "He will be home in five minutes." Immediately a supernatural peace poured over me like billowing waves.

Mother was still praying and crying in the adjacent room. I walked up to her, gently put my arm around her frail body and said, "Mom, Ronnie will be here in five minutes."

She wiped her tear-filled eyes and asked, "How do you know?"

"The Lord told me while I was praying," I responded. "Everything will be all right." And in exactly five minutes Ronnie opened the door and walked into the waiting arms of a teary-eyed mother who was grateful to have her son home safe.

Hezekiah could have thrown up his hands in light of the

troubles he faced. He could have given up, but he turned to God in prayer and waited for God to rescue him in his hour of trouble.

On many occasions during the course of my life I could have given up, and at times, for a brief moment, I have entertained the thought. But when I cried out to God in faith, believing that He could and would deliver me in my time of need, God has always been faithful. He has sustained me and carried me through every trial. And even more, He has given me the grace to go on when there seemed to be no other way.

Many times during my concert ministry I have sung a song titled "When Answers Aren't Enough, There's Jesus." I have found the words of this beautiful song to be true at many points in my life: when I lost my father as a little boy; when my only brother, who was having serious health and emotional problems, turned to prescription drugs for several years and his problems made him more distant than a total stranger; when my son David was snatched away suddenly because of the irresponsible decision of a drunk driver; when I thought I would never sing again because of a problem with my vocal cords—in my loneliest hours I discovered "when answers aren't enough, there's Jesus! He's the One Who always cares and understands! When answers aren't enough, He's there."[1]

The Bible says that man looks on the outward appearance, but God looks on the heart. Man sees who you think you are and the person you want others to believe you are. But God sees who you are deep within, beneath all the latest fashions and poised, confident exterior. That is the person He loves and is waiting to rescue from trouble in your time of need.

I am delighted to tell you that my brother was eventually rescued from his troubles. Today he has fully recovered from his problems and is back in full-time ministry.

If you are facing a crisis situation, or if troubles and trials are bombarding you from every side, whisper a prayer right now. God's Word promises in Matthew 21:22, "And whatever things you ask in prayer, believing, you will receive." Ask God Almighty, the Creator and Maker of everything (including you) to help you. Just ask in prayer, believing by faith that He will answer—and He will! Allow the Father to be your strength for today and hope for tomorrow.

## CHAPTER 13

# YOU'RE FINISHED!

*I*t looks as if there is a problem with one of your vocal cords," Dr. Ossof said. "Can you see that restriction right there?" he asked, indicating the probable site of the problem.

I turned my head slightly and looked at the screen where he was pointing. Dr. Ossof was a leading specialist in the area of voice-related problems at the Vanderbilt Voice Clinic. Just moments earlier he had skillfully eased a tiny probe with a camera on the end of it down my throat. He had carefully explained the examination procedure step-by-step, reassuring me that the temporary discomfort of the tiny probe would help him diagnose my problem. By shining a strobe light on the outside of my throat, he would be able to view my vocal cords on the screen.

And that was exactly what happened. As he pointed out the specific areas on what appeared to be an X ray of my vocal cords, I watched intently, trying to understand the gravity of the situation.

After the initial inspection of my vocal cords, Dr. Ossof offered a simple explanation to help me understand better. He said that in reality a person's vocal cords are about the size of a thumbnail. He continued to explain that to make a sound, the vocal cords bang together at the rate of approximately five hundred times a second. As he pointed at the screen, he indicated a flattened area that appeared to be different from the rest of the vocal cord. He paused at the flattened area and noted that there appeared to be a restriction in that section.

The nurse standing beside me who was assisting Dr. Ossof added an unsolicited comment in whispered tones: "Your vocal cords look terrible, Mr. Brock."

*What is happening?* I thought, attempting to disregard the nurse's comments while I continued to watch the doctor's animated diagnosis process. I was not accustomed to having *any* health problems. Every physician up to this point in my life had always told me I was in great condition.

But this was quite different and so foreign to me. Here I was, seated in an examination chair in one of the nation's leading voice specialist's offices with a cameralike probe stuck down my throat! Why, you ask? With absolutely no warning, my voice had all but vanished overnight. As a singer and minister of the gospel, I depended almost totally on my voice, so I needed some answers—and I needed them soon!

## I'M SPEECHLESS!

Let me share a little background with you regarding how this all came about. I spent a weekend in late May of 1996 ministering at a church in Virginia. During that weekend I developed a problem with my throat. With no forewarning I awoke one morning and discovered that I could barely speak. And when I did my customary warm-up exercises of vocal scales and the like, I found that I had almost no voice at all for singing.

At first I didn't give much thought to the matter. I assumed that my throat problems could somehow be attributed to the fact that I had slept under an air-conditioning vent the previous night. Obviously, the air had been blowing directly on me as I slept. In addition, my concert schedule had been very hectic and had included an excessive amount of travel, which was physically exhausting. Therefore, if my voice was as tired as my body felt, it was not surprising that I had a little problem like this, especially with the cold air having blown on me all night.

I tried to dismiss the problem from my mind and did my best to make it through that weekend in Virginia. I did what I usually did under these circumstances: drank hot tea and honey and tried all the home remedies that singers often use. However, all the hot tea, honey, and home remedies combined brought no improvement to my voice.

As a result, I was forced to cancel the following weekend of services that I had scheduled in California. I had been looking forward to being with my dear friend in San Jose, Pastor Kenny Foreman, but there was just no way I could make it. He was so gracious and understanding when I told him I might have to cancel. He told me to take care of myself and get better, reassuring me that we could always reschedule when I had an open weekend in the future.

I pampered my voice throughout the week as I usually did when I had a problem. I continued to drink hot tea with honey and lemon and got some much needed rest. But even with that, there was still no improvement, and I was forced to cancel the second weekend in a row.

At about the same time, I was scheduled to be on TBN's *Praise the Lord* television program with Paul and Jan Crouch. Because I still had no voice, I had no choice but to call Paul and cancel because I just couldn't sing. He was very understanding and graciously released me from my commitment.

My schedule for the following week included a convention in Nashville, Tennessee. Just a few weeks earlier, at approximately the time my voice disappeared, I had run into an old friend named Bill Morris. Bill, also a singer, told me about a specialist named Dr. Ossof at the Vanderbilt Voice Clinic and encouraged me to see him if the problem continued. Bill informed me that this doctor had been written up in *People* magazine, and had served as the physician to a number of singers and speakers, including many of Nashville's top country-and-western stars.

Because my voice was my livelihood, I was getting more and more concerned. It had been three weeks since the problem began, and with no voice, there were no singing or preaching engagements—and that meant no income. I knew I couldn't continue like this, and I thought that a specialist in the field might be able to offer some suggestions. Since I was scheduled to be at a convention in Nashville, and since Dr. Ossof was located in Nashville, I decided to try to get an appointment with him.

Bill had indicated that it might be very difficult to get an appointment with Dr. Ossof, but when I called, my appointment was scheduled for June 14. I made the necessary arrangements to fly to Nashville for the day.

The examination wasn't exactly pleasant, especially when Dr. Ossof eased that probe down my throat, but I was desperate for answers. My desperation and concern made me a very cooperative and willing patient.

During the exam Dr. Ossof asked some questions and pointed out some things on the display screen that was connected to the probe. From time to time he moved the probe in my throat slightly to get a view from several different angles. As he moved the probe around, he provided a narrative of what was being depicted on the screen. Once or twice he directed my attention to specific areas of interest contrasting his findings with what was typical for most individuals. Eventually, he concluded his examination and removed the probe. What a welcome relief that was!

Having completed the examination, Dr. Ossof told me that there was a restriction on my vocal cords and that my voice needed total rest. In addition he said I would have to eliminate all caffeine from my diet because caffeine tends to aggravate this condition. This meant eliminating coffee, soft drinks containing caffeine, and even orange juice as that, too, contains some caffeine. He gave me strict orders regarding the caffeine and the rest, telling me that only time would tell if this approach would help eliminate the problem. Before I left, he told me to come back in late July to determine whether or not the rest and changes he had prescribed had been of any help.

## THERE'S NOTHING LEFT!

As I flew home later that day, I wondered what was ahead. I really had no more answers than I had when I came, and the information Dr. Ossof did provide painted a fairly grim picture. And I must admit, I was somewhat depressed and struggling with doubt. I had faced problems in life, but none like this—and my voice was absolutely vital to my career as a preacher and singer.

*How am I going to make it?* I thought as I sat in the airplane headed for home. *What am I going to do?* After all, I had responsibilities and commitments to keep. What about all the pastors who were expecting me to minister in their churches in the next few weeks? What about the upcoming weekend? Then there was the crusade in Louisville with Benny Hinn. It was just a few weeks away, and I had to be there; these crusades had become a part of my life, and I looked forward to each one with great expectation. I couldn't bear to think of the alternatives. If I couldn't sing and preach, what did I have left?

These questions tormented me throughout my flight. And mixed in with the questions were the harassing words of the enemy of my soul. These destructive, haunting words began to ring in my mind again—and they were all too familiar. "I've got you now. I took your father, I took your brother, I took your son, and now I've taken your voice. It's over! I've finally got you—you'll never preach another sermon or sing another song. You're finished!"

I tried my best to deal with the barrage of attacks, but it was difficult because the familiar words that were assaulting my mind were haunting and powerful. I tried to ignore the harassing, sneering words of the enemy and focus on what Dr. Ossof had said to me just before I left his office: "I want to see you in a month. Until then, rest your voice. Avoid using it as much as possible."

Although I was extremely troubled about the uncertainties of the future, I was relieved that Dr. Ossof had told me to rest my voice. That meant I didn't have to talk to anyone, and I didn't feel like talking anyway. I had nothing to say because my mind was totally occupied with negative thoughts of worry and doubt.

## PRAY, MOM!

I fretted about the future all the way home from Dr. Ossof's office. I was filled with turmoil, and I had so many questions. But unfortunately, I had no answers!

Despite the problem with my voice and all the snarling lies that Satan continued to hurl my way, I knew that prayer was my only recourse. I knew I could take my problems to the Lord because the Bible was filled with such promises:

*God is our refuge and strength,*
*A very present help in trouble.* (Psalm 46:1)

*Cast all your anxiety on him because he cares for you.*
(1 Peter 5:7 NIV)

*For with God nothing will be impossible.* (Luke 1:37)

*I am the LORD who heals you.* (Exodus 15:26)

With these promises from God's Word to cling to, I turned to God for the answer.

And as I had always done when I faced a crisis, I called my mother. I explained in detail to her what had happened to my voice and what the doctor had told me. Then I asked her to pray. She had always been such a prayer warrior. Ever since I could remember, I had witnessed the results of her prayers.

Her relationship with the Lord was special, and on many

occasions when she interceded for specific prayer requests, the Lord would sometimes speak to her through Scripture. And that's what happened when she began praying for me and my voice problem.

Not long after my call, I received a letter from her containing a number of Scriptures that really helped to build my faith. Psalm 91 was one portion of Scripture that she directed me to read. As I read it, I made it personal and began to declare the Word of God over my life. Here is the passage, as I personalized it for me:

> I will dwell in the secret place of the Most High
> And abide under the shadow of the Almighty.
> I will say of the LORD, "He is my refuge and my fortress;
> My God, in Him I will trust."
> Surely He shall deliver me from the snare of the fowler
> And from the perilous pestilence.
> He shall cover me with His feathers,
> And under His wings I shall take refuge;
> His truth shall be my shield and buckler.
> I shall not be afraid of the terror by night,
> Nor of the arrow that flies by day,
> Nor of the pestilence that walks in darkness,
> Nor of the destruction that lays waste at noonday.
> A thousand may fall at my side,
> And ten thousand at my right hand;
> But it shall not come near me.
> Only with my eyes shall I look,
> And see the reward of the wicked.
> Because I have made the LORD, who is my refuge,
> Even the Most High, my dwelling place,
> No evil shall befall me,
> Nor shall any plague come near my dwelling;
> For He shall give His angels charge over me,
> To keep me in all my ways.
> In their hands they shall bear me up,
> Lest I dash my foot against a stone.
> I shall tread upon the lion and the cobra,

*The young lion and the serpent I shall trample underfoot.*
*I will set him on high, because he has known My name.*
*Steve shall call upon Me, and I will answer him;*
*I will be with him in trouble;*
*I will deliver him and honor him.*
*With long life I will satisfy him,*
*And show him My salvation.*

In that same letter my mother also directed my attention to Psalm 94:4–11. As I read these words, they almost jumped off the page at me.

*They utter speech, and speak insolent things;*
*All the workers of iniquity boast in themselves.*
*They break in pieces Your people, O LORD,*
*And afflict Your heritage.*
*They slay the widow and the stranger,*
*And murder the fatherless.*
*Yet they say, "The LORD does not see,*
*Nor does the God of Jacob understand."*
*Understand, you senseless among the people;*
*And you fools, when will you be wise?*
*He who planted the ear, shall He not hear?*
*He who formed the eye, shall He not see?*
*He who instructs the nations, shall He not correct,*
*He who teaches man knowledge?*
*The LORD knows the thoughts of man,*
*That they are futile.*

The familiar words "You're finished!" that I had heard in my mind revealed that the enemy was involved and that this was a fight to the finish. Knowing this, I began to prepare for battle!

## A CALL TO ARMS

The Christian's life is at times a life of warfare and spiritual conflict. In Ephesians 6:10–18 Paul depicts the Christian facing a foe and being forced into warfare. It is an inevitable consequence of a life lived in Christ, because we are walking as foreigners through a world that "lies under the sway of the wicked one" (1 John 5:19) and is under his domination.

Knowing this, Paul gives us a call to arms. Ephesians 6:10–11 says, "Finally, my brethren, be strong in the Lord and in the power of His might. Put on the whole armor of God, that you may be able to stand against the wiles of the devil."

The word *finally* implies a climax to the epistle. Paul is addressing his "brethren." He is speaking not only to fellow apostles or fellow pastors and evangelists, he is speaking to you and to me. The archenemy of Christ is attacking His body, of which the brethren are members. No one is exempt from the conflict.

"Be sober, be vigilant; because your adversary the devil walks about like a roaring lion, seeking whom he may devour" (1 Peter 5:8).

In this verse the devil is compared to a roaring lion. Have you ever watched a documentary on television about the lion? He is often referred to as the "king of the jungle," a name that did not come to him by accident! The lion is strong, forceful, fierce, and ferocious, words that at times could also describe our cunning foe, the devil.

Just like the lion, the devil attacks ferociously and forcefully. The lion's attacks are relentless and repeated until he has conquered his prey or until the prey has escaped. So it is with the enemy of our soul who always comes only to steal, kill, and destroy. On many occasions he has tried to subdue and conquer me by boasting of his seeming victories. His haunting words harassed me: "It's over! I took your father, your brother, your son, and now I've taken your voice! I've got you! You'll never preach another sermon or sing another song. You're finished!"

As the devil's crippling blow of fear was about to be delivered, I began to recognize the cunning ways of my foe. By attempting to take my voice, my future as a preacher and a singer was not all that was at stake. If my voice was impaired, I would not be able to tell others about God's love or His plan of redemption through Calvary. If I could not speak, I would be unable to show others how to "stand against the wiles of the devil" by putting on the whole armor of God (Ephesians 6:11). Without my voice, I couldn't warn teenagers to stay away from alcohol and drugs. Without my voice, I couldn't unmask the enemy who goes about as a roaring lion, seeking to devour anyone he can. My struggle was one that went beyond the natural realm. It was a conflict with which Paul was acquainted.

Paul accurately describes the conflict when he declares we are wrestling. "For we do not wrestle against flesh and blood, but against principalities, against powers, against the rulers of the darkness of this age, against spiritual hosts of wickedness in the heavenly places" (Ephesians 6:12). The antagonists are strong, and we are in a desperate, hand-to-hand battle. The conflict is not with the human and the visible realm, but with the invisible.

Paul tells us that our wrestling match is not with flesh and blood but with invisible principalities (the power, spirit, and principles of a tyrant); against powers (demons put at his charge, or master spirits); against rulers of this present darkness; and against the spirit forces of wickedness in the heavenly supernatural sphere.

The names given to the devil are an indication of his personality: Satan, deceiver, liar, murderer, accuser, tempter, prince, *Apollyon* ("destroyer"), the evil one, Beelzebub. Each name is repulsive and discloses something about his nature.

I have encountered his lying, deceiving ways in the past. In myself and in my own strength, I was no threat to him. But with the Lord on my side, Satan—the evil one—could not stand. His lies crumbled and his accusations evaporated as Jesus Christ came on the scene. Through His divine intervention from the throne room of heaven, the Lord and I were a majority, and Satan was subdued.

# A SERMON FROM MY SON

As parents, we spend years of our lifetime trying to instill good values, principles, and understanding in our children. As Christians, we dedicate ourselves to training them in the ways of the Lord, endeavoring to instruct them in the principles taught in the Bible. Through these biblical principles, we attempt to prepare them for life here on earth and also for life eternal. We try to set a good example before them through our own lives. In fact, at times we may even preach to them!

But what a strange thing it is to change places with them and *listen* to a sermon rather than deliver one. That's exactly what happened to me.

One day shortly after my visit to Dr. Ossof's office, Tony and Gwen were at our house. Pat, Tony, Gwen, and I were all sitting around the table having a family devotional together. During our devotional, Tony began to speak. He knew that because of the problem I was having with my voice, I was extremely concerned about the uncertainty of the future.

He began by saying, "What about Philippians 4, Dad? Have you thought about that portion of Scripture lately?" Then he reached for his Bible and began to read these words:

> *Be anxious for nothing, but in everything by prayer and supplication, with thanksgiving, let your requests be made known to God; and the peace of God, which surpasses all understanding, will guard your hearts and minds through Christ Jesus. (Philippians 4:6–7)*

Tony glanced at me for just a moment and then continued. "Dad, look at what this says." And with that he pointed to the notations and reference remarks alongside the verse. "The study notes for those two verses say 'Supplication is more than petitioning, but suggests an intensity of earnestness in extended prayer—not to gain merit by many words, but to fully transfer the burden of one's soul into God's hands. Prayer and peace are closely connected. One who entrusts cares to Christ instead of fretting over them will experience the peace of God to guard him from nagging anxiety.'" He laid his Bible down on the table and turned toward me again. It was obvious that he had strong feelings regarding what he was about to say. "Dad, that's you," he said, pointing to the reference notes he had just read to me. "You've been fretting . . . you've been fretting over this problem with your voice. In fact, I think that somehow your fretting has something to do with David."

The truth of Tony's words and the two verses from the Bible hit me right between the eyes. I had not turned all my cares over to the Lord. Losing David in such a sudden and tragic way still tormented me from time to time, even though it had been several years since his death. Now the problem with my voice seemed to give Satan even more opportunity to harass me. Granted, I had asked my mother to pray for my voice problem when Dr. Ossof gave me his diagnosis, and I sincerely believed that God heard her prayers. But I had not released my cares to the Lord. Therefore, I had no peace but just the nagging anxiety that Tony had mentioned.

We concluded our devotional time, and Tony and Gwen said good night and left. Throughout the remainder of the evening and in the days that followed, Tony's words kept coming back to me. I read and reread the verses from Philippians that he had pointed out to me. I was continually drawn back to those verses. Each time I read that portion of Scripture, my faith became stronger and bolder. I could sense that something was happening too! My faith was increasing, and I had an inner confidence that dispelled any doubts I had once known.

As my faith increased, I began to release my cares to the Lord just as Tony had said. As I cast my cares upon the Lord and made my requests known to God in prayer, that peace that passes all understanding came just as it was promised in Philippians 4:6–7. Although nothing had changed in the natural realm, the anxiety that had consumed me was gone! The problem with my voice still remained the same, but the anxiety about my voice and my future was now gone—it had been replaced with a peace that was beyond anything I had ever imagined possible!

## GIVE ME THE PAIN; YOU KEEP DAVID

A few days later while I was in prayer, the Lord revealed a marvelous truth to me that began to bring healing to my wounded heart. Looking back now, I believe it was actually prompted by Tony's sermon to me on fretting. First, the Lord showed me that I had been fretting over losing David for the past several years. In Psalm 37:8, *The Living Bible* says, "Stop your anger! Turn off your wrath. Don't fret and worry—it only leads to harm."

In that tender time of prayer, I began to understand what a subtle impact the fretting really had upon my life and my state of mind. As a result, I had become more vulnerable to the lies of Satan and perhaps less aware of the source. And now those lies had begun to take a great toll on every area of my life.

As I continued in prayer, the Lord also showed me that on many occasions I had actually felt a sense of guilt about David's death. As I prayerfully considered this more closely, I began to realize that this was true, because deep down inside, I felt guilty because David was dead and I wasn't. After all, I was the father, the protector, the provider, the invincible one, and it was my duty before God and to my family to protect them and shelter them from any harm. But I had failed, and David was dead!

And I had believed the lies of Satan when he spewed out his destructive words, "You're a loser!" because I actually saw myself as a failure too.

As the truth of my long bout with fretting and guilt began to unfold before me, I heard my heavenly Father gently whisper these loving words to my heart, "Give Me the pain, you keep David."

In that moment of time I felt almost like a blind man whose sight had suddenly been restored. Like Bartimaeus, a glorious transformation of my world had taken place and suddenly changed from darkness to light. As my spiritual eyes of understanding began to see beyond the visible into the invisible realm, I realized that I had believed a lie. In my pain and sorrow I had mistakenly believed that the only way I could hold on to David was to embrace the pain I associated with his death. But now I realized that was not so.

Suddenly the scales had been removed from my eyes, and I recognized that this had been a subtle and deceptive ploy of the evil one. I hadn't really lost my son David, for death is not a dead end that leads to nowhere, but a doorway to eternity. David and I had only experienced the temporary separation that death brings. Oh, yes, he was gone from this earth and from me, and I would never hug him or laugh with him again here on earth, but I had the glorious assurance that he was waiting for me just inside those pearly gates. I hadn't lost David, because we would spend eternity together around the throne of God.

I bowed my head and from the depths of my heart whispered a prayer of thanks to the Lord. As I did, I remembered Tony's sermon to me at the kitchen table only days before.

*Be anxious for nothing, but in everything by prayer and supplication, with thanksgiving, let your requests be made known to God; and the peace of God, which surpasses all understanding, will guard your hearts and minds through Christ Jesus.*
(Philippians 4:6–7)

With my anxiety gone and my newfound peace from above, I started to see my surroundings in a different light. Instead of fretting about my failures and worrying about my vocal cord problems, I began to recognize some of the blessings that had been there all the time, blessings that I had overlooked up until this time: my wonderful wife, Pat, Tony and Gwen, my beautiful grandchildren who are the light of my life and whom I adore, my family and friends, and so much more. I started to appreciate what I had instead of mourn over what had been taken from me.

I'll never forget that day, for it was the first time since that terrible phone call in July of 1986 that I actually felt that there was hope for tomorrow. And I was ready to start walking and living in that glorious hope.

# CHAPTER 14

## A
## BRIGHT,
## NEW DAY!

The next morning I opened my eyes to discover a beautiful, new day. Today was different. The dread of facing another day that had become so commonplace with me was now just a vague memory—*almost* as if it never happened! I was grateful to be alive!

Pat had awakened early, and it was apparent that she already had made the morning coffee. The aroma of the freshly brewed coffee beckoned to me as it drifted into the bedroom. I slowly pushed back the covers, got out of bed, and made my way toward the kitchen.

I walked over to the cupboard, opened the door, and reached for a coffee mug. As I placed the mug on the counter, I heard Pat's voice behind me. "Steve, remember what Dr. Ossof said. You're not supposed to have caffeine."

Her words quickly brought to mind the problem with my vocal cords and the uncertainty of what lay ahead. Worry and fear raised their ugly heads immediately, trying to displace the peace that filled my heart today. At the same time, Tony's text that was found in Philippians 4:6–7 from the "kitchen table sermon" came to mind.

"Be anxious for nothing, but in everything by prayer and supplication, with thanksgiving, let your requests be made known to God; and the peace of God, which surpasses all understanding, will guard your hearts and minds through Christ Jesus" (Philippians 4:6–7).

I knew that much of the anxiety, along with the fretting that had stalked my thoughts almost every waking moment, had miraculously left me. And I was truly trying to be thankful for the blessings in my life. But the nagging question of what lay ahead was still there. I still hadn't been able to resume my concert or speaking schedule due to the problems with my vocal cords. I was following Dr. Ossof's orders, but would it be enough? What would he find when I returned for my follow-up visit? And then there was the Louisville Miracle Crusade with Benny Hinn—that was only days away! Concern gripped me as I pondered the somewhat dark, uncharted road ahead. What was going to happen?

## THE CURE FOR WORRY

It's easy to tell someone else, "Don't worry," but when the problems are yours and you're the one doing the worrying, it's not quite that simple. The uncertainty seems to linger in your mind, and worry is always waiting just around the corner, ready to displace any measure of faith and overtake an unsuspecting victim.

The Bible has much to say about worry. There is probably no command found in Scripture that is broken more often than the one found in Philippians 4:6, "Be anxious for nothing, but in everything by prayer and supplication, with thanksgiving, let your requests be made known to God."

How many individuals are caught in the trap of worry, and experience great anxiety over the unknown? You probably know several. Perhaps you are also caught in this trap. If so, do you long to be free from the exhausting grasp of that anxiety?

The penalty for profuse worry is inescapable. From brooding over anxieties the mind becomes exhausted, the spirit gets depressed, the body grows exceedingly weary, and worst of all, the cares of life remain squarely upon your shoulders, weighing you down. In your own strength, this load is too great to bear.

Philippians 4:6 not only directs you and me not to tolerate worry and anxiety, but it also reveals the remedy: prayer. It's not always easy to do, but we are to pray about the things that concern us and give thanks. This verse obviously includes every area of life, for no exclusions are listed.

Jesus said, "Which of you by worrying can add one cubit to his stature?" (Matthew 6:27). Think about it for a moment. What does worry really accomplish?

Worry has never yet brought healing from cancer or any other disease, it has never rescued a business from financial peril, nor prevented a national disaster or personal tragedy. Worry and anxiety are actually powerless in bringing about change or producing anything positive. Yet, they have the power to emotionally cripple and bind an individual.

Dr. Billy Graham once said,

> Historians will probably call our era "the age of anxiety." Anxiety is the natural result when our hopes are centered in anything short of God and His will for us. When we make anything else our goal, frustration and defeat are inevitable. Though we have less to worry about than any previous generation, we experience more worry. Though we have less real cause for anxiety than our forefathers, we are inwardly more anxious. In days gone by calloused hands were the badge of the pioneer, but a furrowed brow is the insignia of today's modern man.
>
> God has never promised to remove all our troubles, problems, and difficulties. In fact, sometimes I think the truly committed Christian is in conflict with the society around him more than any other person. Society is going in one direction, and the Christian is going in the opposite direction. This brings about friction and conflict. But God has promised, in the midst of trouble and conflict, a genuine peace, a sense of assurance and security, that the worldly person never knows.[1]

That day in Nashville when I heard Dr. Ossof say, "Your voice needs total rest, and if things don't change, you may have to stop singing," so many thoughts raced through my mind, thoughts of anxiety and worry. In my heart of hearts, I knew that I could trust the Lord for every need, just as I always had. But anxiety and worry attacked my mind as the enemy of my soul whispered those familiar lies from the past: "There's no way you'll climb this mountain. I've really got you this time! Without your voice, you'll never preach another gospel message or sing another gospel song. I've finally silenced you—you're finished!"

Philippians 4:7 held an important key for me. "And the peace of God, which surpasses all understanding, will guard your hearts and minds through Christ Jesus."

Although the doctor had diagnosed a problem on my vocal cords, my mind experienced a greater problem, for it was a great battlefield for worry and anxiety that day in the doctor's office as well as in the days that followed. Yet, no matter how much Satan tried to shout lies like "You're finished" in my ear, the peace of God truly kept my heart and mind.

In my hour of need, I had a measure of faith. That measure of faith wasn't very big, but it was enough. You see, the amount of faith required for God to move mountains is very small. As the Bible states in Matthew 17:20, "If you have faith as a mustard seed, you will say to this mountain, 'Move from here to there,' and it will move; and nothing will be impossible for you."

The situation with my voice was one of the biggest mountains I had ever encountered, second only, I think, to losing David. Yet, I knew that no matter what trials I faced, God could sustain me. He had shown Himself strong on my behalf on many other occasions, especially when David was taken from me so suddenly. This was certainly a great opportunity for the Lord to come through again for me because there was really nothing I could do but wait and trust Him.

On many occasions I have heard Benny Hinn say, "Miracles begin when abilities cease." In other words, do everything you can in the natural realm—pursue every avenue that potentially could hold the answer to your situation—and then trust God to do the miraculous.

That's exactly what I did, both in the natural and in the spiritual realms. All the while I was trusting the Lord Jesus for my miracle, I did everything I could to follow the doctor's orders, using my voice as little as possible. I rested my voice, changed my diet, canceled every possible engagement I could, and I waited.

In the spiritual realm I allowed the peace of God to keep my heart and mind as I made my requests known to God in prayer. I trusted God while I used the weapons of spiritual warfare as identified in 2 Corinthians 10:4–6:

> *For the weapons of our warfare are not carnal but mighty in God for pulling down strongholds, casting down arguments and every high thing that exalts itself against the knowledge of God, bringing every thought into captivity to the obedience of Christ.*

I put on the whole armor of God as recorded in Ephesians 6:13–18 to fight the battle that was in the spirit realm: my struggle with worry and anxiety:

> *Therefore take up the whole armor of God, that you may be able to withstand in the evil day, and having done all, to stand. Stand therefore, having girded your waist with truth, having put on the breastplate of righteousness, and having shod your feet with the preparation of the gospel of peace; above all, taking the shield of faith with which you will be able to quench all the fiery darts of the wicked one. And take the helmet of salvation, and the sword of the Spirit, which is the word of God; praying always with all prayer and supplication in the Spirit, being watchful to this end with all perseverance and supplication for all the saints.*

I also trusted God and had faith in His promises. During my years of ministry I had preached eloquent sermons from many different pulpits on the promises of God. I had quoted many of God's promises found in Scripture to others in times of need or crisis. Now it was time for me to believe and apply these promises in my own life—promises like the one in Matthew 21:22, which says, "And whatever things you ask in prayer, believing, you will receive."

The Bible also states,

*Ask, and it will be given to you; seek, and you will find; knock, and it will be opened to you. For everyone who asks receives, and he who seeks finds, and to him who knocks it will be opened. Or what man is there among you who, if his son asks for bread, will give him a stone? Or if he asks for a fish, will he give him a serpent? If you then, being evil, know how to give good gifts to your children, how much more will your Father who is in heaven give good things to those who ask Him!* (Matthew 7:7–11)

Although I didn't know what the future held, I did know that God is a good God who gives good things to His children. I knew His promises were true and that they were for me right now. Although it was difficult to see the future in a positive light, I knew that no matter what unknowns lay ahead, they were really opportunities for God to demonstrate His love and care toward me as my heavenly Father by rescuing me in my hour of need.

## THE FATHER'S CARE

I read a story several years ago about some little children who were trapped in a burning building. Although I don't recall where I read it, the message of the story remains very clear in my mind. All the passageways to where the children were located in the burning building were blocked by the raging flames. As the flames engulfed more and more of the burning building, the children were forced to flee to the ledge of a window on the top story of the building. There was no way of escape for the children and no way for the firemen to reach the area where the children were trapped.

As a last resort, the firemen rigged up some outstretched blankets below the window ledge where the children were. As they held the blankets tightly, the firemen called out to the children and encouraged them to jump into the blanket. For some time the firemen urged them to jump to safety, but to no avail. The children wouldn't budge from the window ledge, even though the flames were getting closer and closer all the time.

Suddenly, a man came running down the street. As he rounded the corner, he looked up at the window ledge and saw the children huddling helplessly together. He ran quickly toward the place where the firemen were holding the outstretched blanket. He called the first child by her name and yelled, "Jump! They'll catch you." Without hesitating, the little child leaped from the ledge to safety below. She was quickly snatched from the blanket. Immediately the man spoke another name and yelled, "Jump" once again. The little boy up on the ledge responded immediately by leaping into the awaiting blanket below.

Onlookers began to inquire why the children so readily responded to this man's cry and not to the cries of the firemen who had tried for several minutes to rescue the children. "What is your secret?" they asked. "Why did they jump at your command but not for the firemen?"

"I'm their father," the man responded. And with that he knelt on the sidewalk and put his arms around his children, caressing them lovingly.

When the father told his children to jump, they had confidence to believe that what he said was true and that everything would be all right. Without hesitation, they believed his word and acted upon it. If natural children can trust their earthly father with such perfect faith, we should never hesitate to believe or act upon the word of our heavenly Father.

Our heavenly Father says to every believer, "My promises will never fail. I will never let you down, I will never forsake you." Deuteronomy 31:8 promises "And the LORD, He is the One who goes before you. He will be with you, He will not leave you nor forsake you; do not fear nor be dismayed." And what

God has promised, He is able to perform. He says whatever you need can be found and supplied through Him. "And my God shall supply all your need according to His riches in glory by Christ Jesus" (Philippians 4:19).

Regardless of what your needs are, remember that God has everything you need. If God is limited, it is because you have limited Him through your unbelief.

## THE BURDENS OF LIFE

My concerns became somewhat of a burden for me to bear when there was no apparent change in the condition of my voice. But then I knew that life brings real burdens to all of us at times. Perhaps it's your daily work or the duties of home, raising your children or financial difficulties. Perhaps it's growing older and watching your strength decrease with the years. But no matter what burden may be weighing heavily upon you today, the question that still remains is: Are you going to bear the burden alone? You don't have to, but the choice is yours.

The cure for worry lies not in ignoring our burdens but in casting them upon the Lord in prayer. Once you have cast your cares upon the Lord, one of the greatest challenges you may face is not taking them back.

We cast our cares upon the Lord as we learn to pray. I learned a secret a long time ago: where there is no prayer there is no peace. So when you face worry, remember these three things:

1. God knows.
2. God cares.
3. God can help.

## God Knows

Trouble will do one of two things to you when it comes knocking at your door: it either moves you toward God or away from Him—the final decision is up to you. Allow the Holy Spirit to teach you how to handle your difficulties so you may profit from them.

Throughout history the greatness of men has been traceable to their difficulties. Often, the greater a man, the greater the dimension of his difficulties. In many ways we are like a precious stone. A gem cannot be polished without friction, nor a man perfected without adversity.

Whatever happens, look for God's hand in the situation, clasp it, and hold on. Just as a child clings to his father's hand in a dark room, confident that his father can safely guide him out of the darkness and into the light, so we should cling to our heavenly Father's hand, allowing Him to carefully guide us through those times that are darkened by worry and anxiety. When we hold fast to our loving heavenly Father's hand, we have nothing to fear, for the light of His glorious love will lead us to safety and peace.

## God Cares

Although the difficulties that you may be facing are not pleasant, remember that God will never leave you. God is concerned about the things that concern you, and longs to take care of you and meet your needs. All you need to do is call upon Him, give Him your cares and worries, and allow Him to take control of every situation. As you do, He will show Himself strong on your behalf and will meet your needs as you trust Him to do so.

> *Therefore I say to you, do not worry about your life, what you will eat or what you will drink; nor about your body, what you will put on. Is not life more than food and the body more than clothing? Look at the birds of the air, for they neither sow nor reap nor gather into barns; yet your heavenly Father feeds them. Are you not of more value than they?* (Matthew 6:25–26)

## God Can Help

Paul said, "Be anxious for nothing." Then he offers this formula for victory: "But in everything by prayer and supplication, with thanksgiving, let your requests be made known to God" (Philippians 4:6).

The key is clearly presented here. Pray and give thanks. Don't lock your troubles up in your heart. Bring them out in the open, and tell God all about your difficulties. Stop dwelling on your problems and start thanking God for the grace to cope with them.

When I stopped focusing on my problems and my pain and began to trust God for the strength to carry on, He met me at the point of my need. He gave me the grace to get through those long, lonely nights. He gave me the strength to go on when I didn't think I could continue for another moment. Because of that grace, I was able to see what I had and not what had been taken from me. My sadness and despair turned to happiness and joy as I was thankful for my blessings.

As Paul advised in the book of Philippians: be careful for nothing; be prayerful in everything; be thankful for anything! You can be carefree without being careless. This is the happy and right way to live.

The Scriptures go on to say that if you will do these things, "The peace of God, which surpasses all understanding, will guard your hearts and minds through Christ Jesus" (v.7).

A wonderful illustration of peace was once given by Martin Luther. Pointing to a little bird one day, he said, "Look how that little fellow preaches faith to us all. He takes hold of his twig, tucks his head under his wing, and goes to sleep, leaving God to care for him." Don't waste your time in worry but learn to cast every care and burden upon the Lord in prayer.

As you cast every care upon the Lord through prayer, the burdens that have been weighing you down roll off, and a divine peace settles in. I have experienced this dimension of supernatural peace, and it is glorious! The peace that God gave to me in the midst of my turmoil was truly beyond my ability to comprehend. As I look back on that day when I had to walk away from David's gravesite, I had no peace. And I didn't think that I would ever know the glorious ecstasy of God's sweet peace again.

But God is faithful, and now—ten years later—I have a peace that passes all understanding. I know that I will see David again some day and be reunited with him for eternity. Together, we will sing and shout and hug one another for a thousand years or more as we stand side by side and look into the loving face of our wonderful Savior, Jesus Christ.

## PEACE IN THE MIDST OF A STORM

This kind of peace is available for every trial. Sometimes it takes longer to arrive, but it does come when we trust God for our needs in prayer.

When I was buffeted on every side during the trial with my voice problems, I needed this kind of peace. I knew it was available because I had experienced it in many other situations. But God had a specific plan, and I was forced to wait for Him to reveal His plans and purposes. That revelation came in Louisville! Let me tell you about it!

## . . . AND THEN LOUISVILLE

As I explained before, I was carefully following Dr. Ossof's orders. I was resting my voice as much as possible, which included canceling the majority of my speaking and singing engagements.

Not long after Dr. Ossof diagnosed my vocal cord problem, I was scheduled to be in Louisville, Kentucky, for the Benny Hinn Miracle Crusade. I was going to do everything I could to be there because I couldn't bear the thought of missing a crusade. They had become part of my life; besides, being in the atmosphere of the miraculous was just what I needed.

I was scheduled to preach at a nearby church the weekend before the Louisville Miracle Crusade. I kept the commitment, but I did everything I could to avoid singing that weekend because I had almost no voice. Even if I could manage to produce a note I did not have my normal vocal range.

I was scared and apprehensive that I wouldn't make it. After all, I was still under doctor's orders to rest my voice as much as possible, and my follow-up appointment with Dr. Ossof was scheduled just days after the Louisville Crusade. I had been abiding by the doctor's orders, but there had been no noticeable improvement. The Louisville Miracle Crusade was just days away, and I knew I had to save my voice as much as possible for it.

I struggled through the weekend and prepared to head for Louisville. I was determined not to miss this crusade, even if I couldn't produce one note. I knew I had to be there. Being around miracles inspires faith to trust God for the miraculous, and this time I was the one in need of a miracle!

## BREAKTHROUGH IN LOUISVILLE

I went to the crusade with a great deal of concern and apprehension. I didn't know what to expect. My role at the crusades each month was as a singer. I sang solos, I sang with Pastor Benny at times and also with Alvin Slaughter. I loved doing it all. I looked forward to each crusade because these crusade services were always the highlight of my month. After being involved month after month with Pastor Benny and his team at the crusades, it was almost like getting together with family.

Each crusade service is different. Much of the music is spontaneous, and I never really know what I will be called upon to do. Prior to the crusade I had an opportunity to tell Pastor Benny about my vocal problem. Since I didn't know what I might be asked to do in Louisville, I felt I had to make him aware of my problem.

He was very gracious and understanding. He expressed his concern for me tenderly and with great sensitivity. He assured me that everything would be all right and encouraged me to trust God for a miracle.

# THURSDAY EVENING

Thursday evening went fine. I sang a little with Alvin, who was also aware of my vocal condition. He helped out by taking the high notes and carrying most of the songs.

Pastor Benny soon moved on to other parts of the service. When it was time for the miracle portion of the service, I took my place at the side of the platform as I always did and introduced each miracle as hundreds upon hundreds of people came forward to tell what God had done for them. Speaking was much less stressful for my voice, and I managed to get through the evening.

# FRIDAY EVENING

Friday evening came, and from the outset the service was different. Pastor Benny was bold, and an incredibly strong sense of God's presence was evident early in the service. At one point Pastor Benny glanced in my direction. Then I heard him say my name and announce a familiar song title. I was being called upon to sing a solo!

I was shocked! I didn't even know if my vocal cords could produce anything that sounded musical. I stood up and walked slowly toward center stage. As the musicians began to play the song (this time in a lower key than usual), I glanced in Pastor Benny's direction. Although I'm not a master at reading lips, that night as I stepped forward, I watched closely as his lips formed these words: "I'm praying for you."

# SATAN, YOU'RE A LIAR!

I'll never forget that night. I felt some apprehension as I stood on the platform of the Louisville Miracle Crusade with Benny Hinn. But I also sensed faith rising up in my heart. I was about to open my mouth to sing, but I didn't know what would come out. Actually, I didn't know if *anything* would come out!

As I continued to walk toward Pastor Benny, the healing power of God shot through me like a bolt of lightning, and in a moment

I felt faith fill my being. As Benny Hinn offered a microphone to me, I accepted it in faith, knowing that God had been true to His promise, "I am the God that healeth thee." In an instant I was transformed from a man who had no vocal strength to a man filled with boldness and power in the Spirit. As I lifted that microphone to my lips, I sang, "Satan, you're a liar . . . you're a liar!" I sang with authority, projecting those words from my lips as though they were arrows shooting out of a bow against the enemy.

As I sang those words over and over, more and more strength rushed through my body. That night in Louisville I climbed the mountain that the enemy had tried to put in my way as I experienced the divine touch of God's healing hand on my vocal cords. I sang with strength and clarity, declaring to the devil before the thousands gathered there, "Satan, you're a liar, you're a liar, you're a liar!"

## THE DOCTOR'S REPORT

On July 25 I returned to Dr. Ossof's office for my follow-up appointment. After a thorough examination he said, "I see the hint of something that *was* there. But there's nothing there now!"

Dr. Ossof gave me a clean bill of health on July 25, but God gave me a clean bill of health on June 23, 1995, because that was *my* day for a miracle—the day I told Satan *he* was finished!

## CHAPTER 15

# *I'M A WINNER!*

## THE TEN-YEAR TREK

**M**y journey during the ten years immediately following David's death took me down a road in life that I never thought I would travel. At the outset, I wondered if this unexpected trip would ever end, for I had never traveled this way before. It was difficult to ascertain where this pilgrimage was taking me, for there were no road signs to guide me as I traveled along.

The itinerary included such places as "Depths of Despair Valley," "The Rain Forest of Tears," "A Field of Broken Dreams," "Pain's Memory Lane," "If Only Avenue," and many other equally unpleasant places

At each stopping place there were indications that other weary travelers had been there before me, but there was no way to determine who had been there or when the last traveler had departed. The roller-coaster ride that carried me along only added to the uncertainty of the journey, for it offered no clues regarding the purpose of the trip. There was also no way to determine how far away the destination was or how much longer

I would be traveling before this unplanned and unpleasant venture would end.

The journey was tiring and seemed endless. I didn't want to be a part of it, but somehow I had boarded this vehicle, and I couldn't get off. I was frightened, confused, and alone. I felt trapped, and I didn't know how to get off. What was I going to do?

In desperation I shouted, "Can somebody help me?"

At first, my cry for help seemed to bounce back at me as if I were in a vacuum. But I was desperate, so I cried out for help again. In the midst of that confusion and uncertainty, I lifted my voice once again and in desperation shouted, "Help me, God!" Suddenly my empty world changed. In a moment's time the eternal King of glory came to my rescue, transforming me from a victim to a miracle in the making!

## CLOSING THE DOOR TO YESTERDAY

At one point in my life, my yesterdays made my tomorrows seem very grim and uninviting. The ability to close the door on the pain and grief of the past was beyond what my own strength could accomplish. I couldn't do it on my own. I needed supernatural help, just as David the shepherd boy did when he was about to face Goliath.

When David was preparing to go and fight Goliath, he didn't look at the natural circumstances. He was not distracted by the towering silhouette of the giant, whose booming voice challenged anyone who had the courage to come and fight him.

As David stood before Goliath, he was not moved by the giant's massive armor or gleaming sword. He disregarded Goliath's mocking words: "You send me a boy with a few little stones and a sling. What kind of challenge is this?"

David's faith and confidence were not in the sling and five stones nor in his ability as a marksman. His faith was in God and in God's ability to deliver him and his people from the bondage of the Philistines.

For quite some time the giants of grief, sorrow, anger, bitterness, and other related emotions dominated my life. I don't know how long it took for me to recognize these things from the past as the tormenting giants they posed in my life, as well as in Pat's and Tony's lives. But when I began to see how destructive their hold was upon me, I cried out to the Lord for help. I knew His love and grace could rescue me from the pit of sorrow that had become so familiar to me.

As I took the first step to close that door to yesterday, a strong, invisible hand of love covered mine, and together we began to shut the door on yesterday's giants. I didn't have to struggle, for the Lord was beside me, helping me, just as He helped the shepherd boy deliver the stone that subdued Goliath.

Years after slaying Goliath, David wrote a beautiful psalm, which is perhaps one of the most familiar of all—the Twenty-third Psalm. Although many people can successfully quote the six verses that make up this psalm, I wonder how many individuals have ever stopped to consider the beautiful message of hope that David penned.

*The LORD is my shepherd; / I shall not want.* (He is my complete direction, I can depend upon His guidance. Everything I need, He can and will supply.)

*He makes me to lie down in green pastures; / He leads me beside the still waters.* (He gives me rest and peace.)

*He restores my soul; / He leads me in the paths of righteousness / For His name's sake.* (He grants forgiveness.)

*Yea, though I walk through the valley of the shadow of death, / I will fear no evil; / For You are with me; / Your rod and Your staff, they comfort me.* (He is a Companion who comforts me.)

*You prepare a table before me in the presence of my enemies; / You anoint my head with oil; / My cup runs over.* (He nourishes me and anoints my life.)

*Surely goodness and mercy shall follow me / All the days of my life; / And I will dwell in the house of the LORD / Forever.* (I have no worries about today or the future; I will be with Him forever.)

## STEPPING-STONES TO FREEDOM

When I read Psalm 23 now, I reflect on the keys I discovered that helped me close the door on yesterday.

When I finally came to the realization that I was trapped by the sorrow of yesterday, I knew I could not escape its hold by my own strength. I had tried for years to deal with my pain, but as the months and years passed, it only intensified, and I could not escape its grasp.

But as I called upon the Shepherd of my life, asking Him to help me do what I could not do in my own strength, He did just as He promised and came to my rescue. I began to realize that there was a way out of my valley of despair and that the light at the other end of the tunnel was really the hope of a better and brighter tomorrow—hope that was only found in Jesus Christ.

Every day thereafter was not always perfect, but I began to realize that I could hang on to the wonderful memories of my son David and let go of the pain. For so long I mistakenly believed that to be impossible, but I found that it was not. Like sheep that stay near their shepherd, I knew if I stayed close to my Shepherd, I could find peace and comfort for today and for tomorrow.

Jesus promised in John 14:16–17, "And I will pray the Father, and He will give you another Helper, that He may abide with you forever—the Spirit of truth, whom the world cannot receive, because it neither sees Him nor knows Him; but you know Him, for He dwells with you and will be in you."

The Comforter was with me, helping me through the times of difficulty. In some of my darkest hours, I came to know the reality of the Holy Spirit's abiding presence as Comforter and Friend.

The Comforter is aware of our pain in times of need. He is our Paraclete, "one called alongside to help." God's Word promises that the Comforter will abide with you forever. Remember, no matter what you're facing, you are not alone.

When I reflect on the past, I recall countless times when the Holy Spirit has been my Comforter, and like Paul, I can say, "My speech and my preaching were not with persuasive words of human wisdom, but in demonstration of the Spirit and of power" (1 Corinthians 2:4).

As the peace and comfort that only the Shepherd can give began to fill my life, I no longer wandered aimlessly along. Instead of focusing on what I had lost, I began to look at the blessings I had—my beautiful wife, Pat, Tony and Gwen, and the two beautiful grandchildren they have given me—Victoria and David Connor—truly blessings that were heaven-sent. I thanked the Lord for each of them and for what they brought to my life. As I did, the future looked even brighter.

As I turned around and walked away from the Field of Broken Dreams, I looked forward to the day when Tony and I would stand side by side with our hearts and hands joined in a common cause: to bring a message of hope and healing to the hurting and hopeless, and to introduce every broken heart we met to the Shepherd, Jesus Christ.

At the writing of this book, this dream has already started to become a reality. Tony and I are ministering together more and more. At times we minister together and on other occasions, we minister independently. As you may know, I minister through sermon and song, and to my delight, Tony has followed in my footsteps. He is taking a message of hope found in Jesus Christ to his generation through an anointed pulpit ministry. He also ministers as a concert soloist. We share a common vision that was birthed through the pain and adversity the enemy of our souls tried to use against us. That shared vision is to join our hearts and hands as hope builders in a hopeless world, pointing the hurting to Jesus Christ, our eternal hope.

I have found that with the Shepherd, the cares of this world dim in the light of His glorious love. As His love overshadows a hurting heart, the broken pieces can and will be mended, bringing hope for a new and better day.

## PRESSING ON

I have made a commitment like Paul when he said, "Brethren, I do not count myself to have apprehended; but one thing I do, forgetting those things which are behind and reaching forward to those things which are ahead, I press toward the goal for the prize of the upward call of God in Christ Jesus" (Philippians 3:13–14).

In these two verses Paul pictures the Christian as a runner who will lose the prize if he stops short of the goal or if he fails to keep his eyes on the goal. The Grecian racecourse was well known to Paul and to all his readers. Therefore, he often used it in illustrating the Christian life. A runner who looks to the left or the right during a race to determine the status of an opponent loses some of his momentum and falls behind his potential.

In this great race of life, the Christian must press forward with his eyes fixed on Jesus Christ, never resting until the great race is won and the prize is obtained.

A good athlete never considers any present attainment sufficient. He constantly refines his skill and style to better himself as an athlete.

A perfect example of this can be seen in the 1996 Summer Olympic Games, which were held in Atlanta, Georgia. Modern-day record holders came to the Olympics with aspirations of winning a medal and setting new world records. This was achieved by a number of Olympic athletes. This was accomplished by a young woman from South Africa who swam in the breast stroke competition and broke her own record by several seconds, finishing far ahead of any other athlete in the event.

Paul was no novice when he wrote to the church at Philippi. He was a man rich in many graces far beyond the experience of most Christians. Yet he still felt that he had not reached the great end of his efforts, for he said, "I do not count myself to have apprehended." In other words, "I have not reached the goal."

Paul did not look at or take pride in anything he had attained, although he could have. As a Jew from the tribe of Benjamin, he had a great heritage. He was one of the greatest scholars of his time and was regarded by many as one of the greatest scholars who ever lived. He was well educated and a great philosopher. As a Roman citizen he was highly esteemed and well respected.

Prior to his conversion experience on the road to Damascus, he proudly presented himself as an enemy of Christ and did everything within his power to bring persecution to the believers of his time. But following his conversion, everything changed. He lived a life of hardship, hazard, and heroism. He traveled from island to island and from continent to continent to proclaim that Jesus was the Christ, the Son of the living God.

In 2 Corinthians we find these words of Paul, which describe some of the hardships he encountered:

> In tribulations, in needs, in distresses, in stripes, in imprisonments, in tumults, in labors, in sleeplessness, in fastings; . . . by honor and dishonor, by evil report and good report; . . . in perils of waters, . . . in perils of my own countrymen, in perils of the Gentiles, in perils in the city, . . . wilderness, . . . sea, . . . among false brethren; in weariness and toil, . . . in hunger and thirst, . . . in cold and nakedness" (6:4–5, 8; 11:26–27).

Yet with all his accomplishments and the marvelous impact he had upon his world, he maintained that he had not reached his goal; he had not accomplished all that he set out to do.

Like Paul, I can say that I, too, have not reached my goal. After David's death, my dreams and goals for the future were put on the shelf for a while. The pain of losing him became the focus of my life for some time, and I could think of nothing else but how much I had lost and how much I missed him.

But today I can say that God has given me strength for today and a bright hope for tomorrow. My vision for the future is greater now than it has ever been, and my desire to help the hurting and the helpless has intensified. Why? Because I know what it is to hurt so bad that you think you can't go on. But with God's help, I know that each day as I awaken, I am truly a miracle in the making.

## FAITH FOR TODAY

I recently came across a statement that I want to share with you: "Unless we forget the past, God can't touch the present." How true this is.

Isaiah 43:18–19 says, "Do not remember the former things, / Nor consider the things of old. / Behold, I will do a new thing, / Now it shall spring forth; / Shall you not know it? / I will even make a road in the wilderness / And rivers in the desert." God has done something marvelous for me! He made a way through my wilderness of sorrow and caused rivers of life to spring up in my desert of despair.

I look at life differently now. Each day, I draw more and more strength from the Lord, and although I still face times when I miss David, I no longer grieve for the things that once were. Instead, I rejoice over the blessings I have. I have a purpose, a message of hope, and a sense of destiny.

## LOOKING AHEAD

We must look forward and not behind us. Paul said, "forgetting those things which are behind . . . I press toward the goal." The memory of things behind may cause distractions and bring about wrong decisions.

On many occasions I've heard Benny Hinn share the following statement about forgetting the past: "You can't drive your car forward if you're constantly looking in the rearview mirror." It's a practical example of what I did for a time. Much like Israel when they remembered the fleshpots of Egypt and turned back,

I allowed the memories from the past to be a distraction until God touched me.

## HOPE FOR TOMORROW

To say the years since David's death have been easy for me would be untrue. But, the harder the battle, the sweeter the victory!

Helen Keller was born blind and deaf, and one would assume that the hardship and trials she faced were overwhelming. Yet she said, "I thank God for my handicaps, for through them I have found myself, my work and my God."

Having left those things that are behind, I now look to the future.

God's Word promises: "But those who wait on the LORD / Shall renew their strength; / They shall mount up with wings like eagles, / They shall run and not be weary, / They shall walk and not faint" (Isaiah 40:31).

I'm thankful for what the Lord has done in my life. The experiences of the past several years have brought me to where I am today. Although it wasn't always easy, God has been with me. He has sustained and strengthened me, and today I am glad to be a living demonstration of Christ's power. His grace has been sufficient to bring me to this point in my life, and I know that it will be sufficient to carry me through today and every tomorrow.

At one time I was hurting and without hope; I had nowhere to turn. But through God's grace and because of His faithfulness to me, His love rescued me, bringing healing and strength for today. And with that strength He gave me bright hope for tomorrow. This hope not only enables me to share God's message of hope with those around me, but it will carry me through each day, to every tomorrow, and beyond the grave into eternity where I will be reunited with my son David, and with my wonderful Lord and Savior, Jesus Christ, to dwell in the glory of God's presence forever.

## CHAPTER 16

# EXCHANGING DESPAIR FOR A DREAM

"Y ou're so wrapped up in the thorns of life that you can't enjoy the roses."

That was me! For years I allowed the pain of life's thorns to flourish. I was so preoccupied with the thorns of life that I failed to realize that the budding, beautiful rose just beyond the thorns was about to bloom and produce a most beautiful fragrance. The hurt and pain caused by these thorns dominated that stage of my life, tormenting me month after month and year after year. Eventually, I was so tormented by the thorns that I was oblivious to the fact that the roses even existed!

## THE MASTER GARDENER

As a minister of the gospel, I was very knowledgeable concerning the message of hope contained within and written upon the sacred pages of the Bible. I knew how to introduce others who were hurting to the Master Gardener. Yet when faced with the thorns of life, I failed to apply God's Word to my own life. Consequently, I was burdened down with life's cares and pain.

I was like the man trudging down the road carrying a fifty-pound sack of potatoes on his back. As he was staggering under the weight of his load, his neighbor drove up alongside him with his wagon and offered him a ride. The man gladly accepted the invitation and climbed up into the wagon.

As he sat down, the kind neighbor who had offered him the ride noticed that the man still had the big bag of potatoes on his back. "Put down your load and rest," the neighbor said to the man in the wagon.

"No sir," he said, shifting the weighty load on his back in an attempt to get more comfortable. Then he added, "It is enough to ask that you carry me without carrying my potatoes too."

In many ways I was like that man. I was guilty of trying to carry my grief and pain when the Bible tells us over and over that Jesus has borne our griefs and sorrows.

Like Paul, I discovered that "My grace is sufficient for you, for My strength is made perfect in weakness" (2 Corinthians 12:9). I had experienced God's grace at so many points in my life. I knew what it was to sense God's love in action on my behalf when I was so dependent on and, at the same time, undeserving of His unfathomable love and grace. I was fully aware that it was God's grace that sustained me that day in the church at David's funeral. It was God's grace that gave me the strength to turn around and walk away from David's grave—one of the most difficult things I have ever had to do. God's grace was with Pat, Tony, and me each step of the way, giving us the strength and courage needed for each day.

## SIMPLE BUT PROFOUND

Pat recently shared a brief quote with me from a poem titled "Ye Weary Wayfarer" by the Australian poet Adam Lindsay Gordon. Although these four simple lines were written more than one hundred years ago, they convey a great truth that I want to share with you:

> Life is mostly froth and bubble,
> Two things stand like stone,
> Kindness in another's trouble,
> Courage in your own.

I can tell you from personal experience that it is much easier to speak a word of kindness to a hurting individual than it is to walk courageously through troublesome times with confidence. As a pastor I had often attempted to encourage the hurting and helpless. But when I was faced with a similar situation, all my words of comfort vanished, and I plummeted to the depths of despair. In the midst of my pain, I felt as if I were drowning in a sea of sorrow and hopelessness.

## DROWNING IN A SEA OF SORROW

During the months and years that followed David's death, Pat and I discovered the reality of 2 Corinthians 12:9—that when we were the weakest, God's grace was there to be a strength for us, to sustain us and lift us up above the circumstances of life.

I shared the details with you in a previous chapter of that first New Year's Day without David. That night, I was so overcome by my grief and sorrow that I felt as if I had to look up to see the bottom. I felt such despair that I didn't want to go on. The memories I had of 1986 were so painful that I was ready to end it all just to be sure that I would never go through another year like that again.

But in my weakest hour, God's grace rescued me from this torment, and I shall be forever grateful to my wonderful Lord for His faithfulness.

This period in our lives was also one of Pat's darkest hours. She didn't say much about what she was going through or the trials she faced at the time, but I've come to learn that silence doesn't necessarily mean that everything is OK.

Losing David had been much more traumatic for her than I realized initially. From all appearances, she seemed to be handling his death as well as could be expected under the circumstances. But that's not what was going on deep inside Pat.

At the outset she focused totally on the loss of David. As time passed, her agony was nearly all-consuming, and she sought a way to handle it. To mask the pain, she threw herself into her work, perhaps thinking that this activity would fill the empty, aching place in her heart.

At the same time, my emotional state was shaky, to say the least, and because I had my own grief to deal with, I failed to notice any signs in Pat's behavior that could have been taken as a subtle cry for help. Aware of my fragile state and knowing me as she does, Pat recognized what was going on inside me. Because of her deep love and concern for me, she chose not to add to my burden and attempted to handle her grief on her own.

Recently she talked openly about that eventful New Year's weekend and the grave concerns she had for me. As a dedicated wife and mother, she said that her whole life was neatly wrapped up in me and the boys. Almost everything about her life was attached to one of us in some way.

She said that losing David had been devastating for her. In addition, she recognized what was going on inside me because she knew me so well, and this only added to her concerns. She felt helpless as she watched me drown slowly in my overwhelming grief. As my feelings of loss grew and my pain intensified, my actions and attitudes toward life announced that I had no desire to go on living. She said everything about my behavior indicated that I was ready to give up.

Every time she saw my lack of interest in life demonstrated in some way, she became more afraid. Because her whole life centered around me and our shared ministry, she said she couldn't imagine what life would be like if I were no longer there for her.

Added to this fear and uncertainty, there was Tony to consider too. He was in his senior year of high school, attempting to deal with David's death as best he could. But he was a silent sufferer much like Pat, keeping as much to himself as possible. Consequently, it was difficult to know exactly what he was going through. She said that looking at the overall situation from the perspective of a wife and a mother, she couldn't understand why I would want to leave her and Tony alone. But the road signs were clearly there, and I was becoming more and more despondent.

In my melancholy state of mind, I failed to realize what was happening. But not Pat! She recognized what was happening, and as she has done so many times throughout our life together, she knelt in prayer.

## NO DISTANCE TO PRAYER

That New Year's Eve, Pat turned to the Lord in prayer, the only source of help and hope she knew. As she prayed and cast her cares and anxieties upon the Lord, a miracle took place three thousand miles away in Seattle. The storm clouds vanished, and the sunshine of God's love broke through the darkness that had filled my life. My sorrow gave way to heaven-sent joy, and as 1987 began, I found the strength to face tomorrow.

## THE FIRST FRAGRANT ROSE

The year 1992 was the beginning of something new for Pat and me. We still struggled from time to time with the sorrow and sadness associated with David's death, but we were learning how to deal with it and were trying to go on.

Early in the year, Tony and Gwen moved to Savannah, Georgia, for him to accept a position as the youth pastor with Coastal Cathedral. Not long after their move, Tony said that he and Gwen had something exciting to tell us. When we heard the news, we could hardly contain ourselves! We were going to be grandparents!

## WAITING FOR VICTORIA

We were ready for some good news, and this certainly qualified! We were excited at the prospect of becoming grandparents. That's probably what made the waiting seem so long.

Month after month we waited and talked about the little blessing who was about to grace our lives.

During this time Pat and I were busy; and we were on the road almost all the time. We maintained our own schedule of special services in churches and also participated in the Benny Hinn Miracle Crusades, which were held in a major U.S. city each month.

Shortly after Tony and Gwen shared their news with us, Pat and I headed out to join Pastor Benny and the crusade team for the next Miracle Crusade. Even though Pat and I were busy traveling, we were never too busy to think about our grandchild, who would be arriving in December. During one of these monthly Miracle Crusades, I can remember Pastor Benny calling me forward. I grabbed my microphone as usual and continued in his direction until I was standing beside him.

"Steve, my friend, how are you tonight?" he inquired.

"I'm just marvelous!" I answered.

Pastor Benny looked at me and smiled. It was obvious that he was relaxed and enjoying himself thoroughly.

I smiled back at him. Then I said, "Have you heard the news?"

"What are you talking about, Steve? What news?" he inquired.

"I'm going to be a grandfather!" I blurted out. As I spoke these words, I smiled a smile that must have burst across the entire lower half of my face and perhaps even shined out through my blue eyes!

"Congratulations, Steve! God is so faithful," he responded as he shook my hand and smiled warmly. The applause from the audience affirmed Pastor Benny's words.

That night I sang of God's faithfulness to me. And in the months that followed, as we waited for Victoria to arrive, over and over again I experienced the reality of one of my favorite hymns, which says,

> *Strength for today and bright hope for tomorrow—*
> *Blessings all mine, with ten thousand beside!*
> *Great is Thy faithfulness, Great is Thy faithfulness,*

*Morning by morning new mercies I see;*
*All I have needed Thy hand hath provided—*
*Great is Thy faithfulness, Lord, unto me!* [1]

## THE COUNTDOWN

When December finally arrived, Pat and I got our things together and headed for Savannah. We were eager to meet our grandchild, and we wanted to be there for the birth—no matter what. Tony and Gwen were so thoughtful and allowed us to share the experience with them.

We had been with them for about a week when the labor pains began. We went to the hospital and waited with them as the contractions got closer and closer: thirty minutes apart . . . twenty minutes apart . . . fifteen minutes—the countdown continued until the baby was about to be born. Then the doctor asked Pat and me to step out of the room while the baby was delivered, promising that we would be notified just as soon as our long-awaited guest arrived.

That was December 8, 1992—the day Victoria Kaitlyn arrived and became the youngest Brock in our family!

I had experienced great pain from the thorns of life during the past five or six years, but, that day, I wasn't aware of the thorns. My heart was filled with the fragrance of a fresh, new rose—her name was Victoria!

## HAPPINESS COMES HOME

I can't begin to tell you how excited I was the day Victoria was born. There she was—Victoria Kaitlyn—our first grandchild! For Pat and me, Victoria's birth represented bright hope for the future. Victoria was the first Brock of the next generation, and her arrival had created a feeling of hope in the air. For the first time since David's death, it seemed as if the rain had stopped and a beautiful rainbow had appeared on the horizon of our lives.

Having a baby girl around was a whole new experience for Pat and me. We had only had boys—busy, active, noise-making units that look for dirt, grease, and grime. Neither Pat nor I could remember them being anything like our beautiful porcelainlike doll named Victoria.

There were a lot of things to get accustomed to. This included the ruffles that are synonymous with having a girl. Then there was the "pink everything" and all the lace! And in addition to all this, we were now grandparents!

As grandparents, Pat and I were naturals from the very start. We quickly became the typical doting grandmother and grandfather who carried several photographs of the "princess." With almost no prompting, we eagerly gave any willing party the opportunity to look at our portable photo gallery. We were also willing to share a play-by-play account of "life with Victoria" at any time of the day or night with anyone who would listen!

The changes that Victoria's arrival brought went beyond the lace and the plastic photo case. Things were different for Pat and me too. It seemed that with Victoria's arrival, Pat and I had found a reason to laugh again. We found ourselves smiling and giggling for no apparent reason, and it felt good!

Victoria gave us a reason to look forward to tomorrow, for every day was new with her. There was no way to predict what might happen in Victoria's life on any given day so we just had to wait and see. We waited eagerly to discover what feat she would master or what new accomplishment would be credited to her that day.

Week after week as she grew and matured, she was always doing something new: mimicking someone or saying a new word or taking a step or two. As we watched her grow, it finally seemed that there was a reason to look forward to tomorrow and to the future.

That hope for the future was heightened even more when Tony and Gwen told Pat and me that another grandchild was on the way! That announcement came about a year after Victoria's birth, and when Tony and Gwen shared this news with us, we were ecstatic! Two grandchildren! We couldn't wait!

# THE ANNOUNCEMENT

"Dad," I heard Tony's familiar voice say as I picked up the telephone. "The doctor says this baby is going to be a boy. Torie is going to have a brother!"

"That's great, Tony," I responded. "I can't wait!"

From that moment on, every time someone would ask any question that related to my family in even the most remote way, I would say, "Victoria is going to have a brother, and I'm gonna have a grandson!" or "The doctor says it's a boy!" I took advantage of every opportunity to let the world know about the anticipated arrival of my grandson.

## MY GRANDSON'S ARRIVAL

Month after month the excitement continued to build as we awaited the arrival of our grandson. The joy that Victoria had brought into my life was nearly beyond description, and I couldn't wait to experience a "double portion"!

I had planned my itinerary to be in the Savannah area around the anticipated due date. Shortly after I arrived, Gwen began to experience some prelabor symptoms so I phoned Pat to let her know that it could be any day. Pat had stayed home to complete some projects in the office, since it is often difficult to predict the arrival of a baby. We had agreed that Pat would do her waiting in the office at home while she worked. As soon as Gwen went into labor, Tony or I was to contact her so she could take the next plane to Savannah.

That call had come around three o'clock on the afternoon of August 23, 1994, and Pat had been bubbling with excitement since Tony called. We had waited for this day for months, and now it was here. Everything was ready, so when Pat hung up the telephone, she grabbed her suitcase and headed for the airport to catch the next plane to Savannah.

## HEADED FOR SAVANNAH

Another grandchild! Pat was excited about the new baby, and as she made her way toward Savannah, she couldn't wait to land

and get off the plane. She would meet me in the baggage claim area as usual and together we would go directly to the hospital.

Her happy thoughts occupied her mind during the trip, and before long, the flight attendant's voice was announcing the final approach. It wouldn't be long now!

\* \* \*

Tap, tap, tap . . . knock, knock.

This is what Pat heard as the commercial airliner she was traveling on came to a stop after it taxied up to the ramp at the Savannah airport. It was nearly 10:00 P.M., and Pat was eager to get off the plane after traveling from Cincinnati.

The seat belt light went off about this time, signaling that the plane had come to a stop. Pat released her seat belt and began to gather her belongings. As she reached for something in the overhead compartment, she heard the same sound again—*knock, knock, knock,* followed by some inaudible words. *What's the commotion?* Pat wondered as she closed the compartment. What was going on outside?

As she prepared to exit the plane, she dismissed the questions and tried to concentrate. She quickly reviewed a mental checklist to be certain that she had all her belongings. *Yes, I have everything,* she thought as she stepped into the aisle. She didn't want to leave anything behind. She wanted everything to go smoothly, for today was a very special day—the day her second grandchild would be born!

## IT'S ABOUT TIME

*Knock, knock, knock* . . . There it was again. That sound coming from outside the plane.

"Ladies and gentlemen," came the announcement over the plane's intercom system. "On behalf of the pilots and our Cincinnati-based flight crew, we want to thank you for flying with us today. We trust that you will enjoy your visit here in Savannah or wherever your final destination may take you."

As soon as the announcement was finished, Pat heard the familiar sound of the exit door opening. *Finally*, she thought as she began to move slowly forward in the aisle.

Her mind was filled with thoughts of Tony and Gwen and, of course, the baby! And she knew that Steve would be very anxious to get to the hospital, so she wanted to get off the plane and down to the baggage area as quickly as possible to avoid any delays.

Suddenly, her happy thoughts were interrupted by the recurring *knock, knock, knock* on the outside of the plane.

"Come on," an excited voice said. "Hurry up!"

There seemed to be some commotion near the exit and someone was certainly in a hurry. *They can't be in any greater hurry than I am*, Pat mused as she took a couple of steps forward.

"Come on . . . [*knock, knock, knock*] . . . hurry up!" the same voice ordered. "Let my wife out! We're having a grandbaby!"

Pat thought, *That voice sounds rather familiar . . . sounds a little like Steve. But then, it couldn't be. We're going to meet in the baggage area just as we always do. It must be my imagination.*

"Let my wife out! Hurry up!" the voice demanded. "Come on, Pat! We've got to hurry! . . . Come on, let's go . . . We're having a grandbaby any minute!"

As Pat turned the corner toward the exit door, she was shocked! I was standing outside the door of the plane waiting for her (and not too patiently, I might add!). I'm sure that from the intense look in my eyes and the rosy-pink tone of my face, she knew I was in a hurry!

Relieved to see Pat at last, I grabbed her hand and pulled her through the doorway as I said, "Let's go, we're having a grandbaby!" Then I turned around and hurried up the ramp, pulling Pat along behind.

"What's going on, Steve?" Pat inquired. "I thought we were going to meet in the baggage claim area."

"Keep walking, Pat," I said with a trace of anxiety in my voice. "I'll explain while we walk. We need to keep moving because I don't think we have much time."

As we hurried toward an awaiting car, I began to offer the promised explanation.

"Everything was going along as expected when Tony called you this afternoon. But tonight, things changed, and the labor pains were coming closer together. Your plane was scheduled to land around 10:00 P.M., but by this time, Gwen's labor pains were just three minutes apart. I raced to the airport to pick you up as soon as your plane landed. I was afraid we might miss the baby's birth if we stuck to our original plans so I had to improvise.

"When I got here your plane had just landed. I hurried to meet you at the gate, but they were taking their time in getting the exit ramp in place. All I could think of was to rush down the ramp and get you out of that plane as quickly as possible. Someone tried to stop me, but I pushed past them and kept going. I didn't care what I had to do. I just didn't want to miss the baby's birth."

## THE RIDE TO THE HOSPITAL

It didn't take us very long to get to the hospital. Although I was already a grandpa, I certainly didn't drive like one that day! We sped along the Savannah streets, and before long we pulled up to the curb outside the hospital entrance.

We jumped out of the car, slammed the doors, and ran into the hospital. Pat followed close behind me as we darted down the long hallways toward the maternity wing.

We had been there only a few minutes when Tony walked into the waiting room. I'll never forget that day—August 23, 1994. As Tony walked toward Pat and me, his eyes were gleaming with excitement, and he had a smile spread across his face from ear to ear.

He came over to where Pat and I were waiting, paused for a

moment, and then looked me straight in the eyes. "Well, he's here. It's a boy!" Tony said. Then he added, "Gwen and I have decided to name him David Connor. Although he'll never get to know his uncle, we wanted to name him after David."

Tony's words surprised me, and for a moment I didn't know what to say. I was thrilled to be a grandfather again, and I was delighted that the baby was a boy. And to name him after David— that was even more special.

I turned toward Pat. She smiled at me and repeated the baby's name, "David Connor." As she said the name, tears welled up in her beautiful brown eyes and slowly escaped, gently rolling down her face.

I just stood there, looking at her as so many thoughts raced through my mind. My heart was filled with such deep emotion; and there was so much to take in at that moment. After a moment of silence, I turned to Pat and said slowly with absolute sincerity, "Pat, we can say David's name in our house once again without the sadness and the pain." As I said these words, warm tears spilled onto my shirt.

Tony took a step toward Pat and me as he squeezed my forearm lovingly and said, "You're right, Dad." And with that, he turned around and disappeared through the doorway, where Gwen and his newborn son, David Connor, were waiting for him.

## SHARING THE MESSAGE OF HOPE

When Pat and I left the hospital that day, we were bubbling with excitement and gratitude to our heavenly Father for our grandson. With David Connor's arrival, we had found another reason to look to the future, and we had a sense of purpose that had been absent far too long.

This hope for tomorrow had begun with Victoria's birth. With David Connor's arrival, the accompanying peace and joy mentioned in Romans 15:13 had come to our lives. "Now may the God of hope fill you with all joy and peace in believing, that you may abound in hope by the power of the Holy Spirit."

The darkness and despair that had once lurked in our hearts and in our home had been replaced by an intense hope. A long-awaited miracle had begun, and a sense of destiny prompted us to find a way to share the good news with the hurting and the oppressed.

## A WORK OF GRACE

As healing came to our hearts and lives, our hope for tomorrow increased. Soon this work of grace was evident in our lives, and hurting people began contacting us.

- "How did you make it?"
- "What sustained you in your grief and loss?"
- "What can I do?"
- "Where can I find help?"

Questions like these became more and more common. But where would it lead?

I once heard Benny Hinn say, "Ministry is born out of adversity." I didn't realize how true those words were at the time, but in the months ahead, I would experience this very thing.

## THE ROAD TO TOMORROW

Recently, while paging through a book by Dr. Robert Schuller titled *The Little Book of Hope*, these words stood out: "Make your suffering a passage, not a dead end."[2]

For years I had been at a dead end of sorrow and despair, and it was going nowhere. But as healing came to our lives and as Pat and I prayed about the future, the Lord whispered a most amazing challenge to our hearts, one that came as a direct result of prayer and the writing of this book.

## AFTER THE MIRACLE

The healing process that God's grace has wrought in my life and in Pat's is a never-ending process. As this healing came to our lives day by day, we began to discover the reality of Benny Hinn's statement from a personal perspective: "Ministry is born out of adversity." Looking back on the trials and adverse circumstances we have faced over the past ten years, we have come to realize two very important things:

1. God loves and cares for us more than we can ever comprehend. The depths and magnitude of His eternal love are always extended and available to mankind.

2. There are many hurting and oppressed people everywhere who need to know about God's infinite love and experience His healing touch upon their hearts and lives.

While writing this book, the Lord whispered a challenge to our hearts: *take this message of hope to hurting and oppressed people everywhere*! The more we prayed about this, the more certain we were that our loving heavenly Father was changing the direction of our ministry. He was giving us a new mandate: we were to become "hope builders"!

## THE BIRTH OF H.O.P.E. BUILDERS

We were challenged at the thought of becoming hope builders for we had faced intense feelings of hopelessness and understood all too well the empty, aimless feelings that come when there seems to be no hope. As Pat and I prayed about the future, this divine inspiration unfolded slowly before us. As we reflected on the years of hopelessness we faced, we remembered our desperate search for solace. In our darkest hours of sorrow, grief, and pain, Pat and I desperately sought help. But we discovered very quickly that no one truly understands unless they have experienced the same kind of loss or sorrow.

When all the pain, the sorrow, and the questions finally ceased, I discovered that the only true source of comfort and help was found in the Lord Jesus Christ. He has given me hope, and as a recipient of this eternal hope, I must take this message to the world. I will become a "H.O.P.E. (Helping Oppressed People

Everywhere) Builder" and declare this message to all who will listen!

Dr. Billy Graham expressed his thoughts on the topic of hope when he said:

> The resurrection of Christ brings hope. The late Emil Brunner once said, "What oxygen is for the lungs, such is hope for the meaning of human life." As the human organism is dependent on a supply of oxygen, so humanity is dependent on its supply of hope. Yet today hopelessness and despair are everywhere. Peter, who himself was given to despair during the episode of Calvary, writes in a triumphant note, "Blessed be the God and Father of our Lord Jesus Christ, who according to His abundant mercy hath begotten us again into a lively hope by the resurrection of Jesus Christ from the dead." There is hope that mistakes and sins can be forgiven. There is hope that we can have joy, peace, assurance, and security in the midst of despair.[3]

We experienced this hope in a very personal way, and we sense a divine mandate to carry this message to a hopeless world that is searching for answers.

## IN SEARCH OF HOPE

The hopelessness of today's society is having a more pronounced effect on our nation than ever before. Men and women desperately search for happiness and peace but fail to find the satisfaction and contentment they seek in life. In a society of such affluence, why is this happening?

In my opinion, the reason we as a nation face problems of such magnitude in the areas of drugs, alcoholism, illicit affairs, child abuse, and so much more is because people have no hope and no peace. They struggle and continue to seek happiness in the world.

But I have walked this painful road of hopelessness, and I can say that the one and only source of hope is Jesus Christ.

While working on the final chapters for this book, I made a

commitment to God Almighty to strive to help and assist people who have gone through similar battles and trials. We experienced our own tragedy when we lost David as a result of the irresponsible act of a drunk driver. The pain and heartache that accompanied this tragedy are beyond description and tormented us for years.

I want to bring hope for the hopeless, provide help for the helpless, strength for the weak, and encouragement for those who are struggling. This is my dream.

For too long, sorrow and pain were in control of my life. I had no strength within to face each day, and I had no desire to go on. Pat was going one direction, and I was coasting along aimlessly in another. I had no hope, no vision for tomorrow. My dreams for the future were nonexistent, for I lived in fear of tomorrow. Nearly destroyed and alone, I was lost in the valley of despair with no way out until Jesus rescued me and changed my destiny.

## MY DREAM AND MY DESTINY

Everything is different now! I have a purpose, a goal, a dream! I have a destiny. And I must declare this message of hope, which is found in Jesus Christ, to the hurting and the oppressed in today's world!

The hopeless can be found anywhere: walking down the corridors of the high school just around the corner, working in an office adjacent to yours, sitting in the church pew beside you on Sunday morning. These individuals are overwhelmed by feelings of hopelessness, and the void deep within cries out for relief, just as I did.

## THE DETOUR

July 27, 1986, was the day hopelessness took up residence in my life. Prompted by an unexpected tragedy, I began a journey to nowhere. On this journey I found that every problem was temporary, no matter how difficult or painful the situation seemed. I came to understand that every valley has its low point.

When you reach that point, there's only one way to go, and that's upward.

## TODAY'S DECLARATION

At one point in my life I had no hope, no purpose, and I didn't want to go on. But "the God of hope has filled me with all joy and peace in believing, and I now abound in hope by the power of the Holy Spirit" (Romans 15:13, modified for emphasis).

I have shared this message many times as I stood beside Benny Hinn at a Miracle Crusade. And one of my favorite times in these wonderful crusades is when I hear Pastor Benny call for Alvin Slaughter and Steve Brock. Let me paint the picture for you as if you were sitting there in that arena too.

## "COME AND TAKE YOUR MICROPHONES, GENTLEMEN"

Alvin and Steve look at each other knowingly as Pastor Benny says, "Satan, you're a liar!"

The musicians quickly change to the proper key as the lights are lowered just enough to allow the spotlights to draw the attention of everyone present to center stage. Alvin glances in Steve's direction, smiles, and pulls the microphone to his lips. As the colored lights flicker and change from subtle hues of blue, amber shapes dance across the platform and take over the positions just vacated by the blue tones.

Alvin begins to sing the familiar lyrics of "Praise the Lord"

> When you're up against a struggle
> That shatters all your dreams,
> When your hopes have been cruelly crushed
> By Satan's manifested schemes . . .

As Alvin continues, he sings with determination and conviction, as if he were reflecting on a time when "Satan's manifested schemes" were raging against his life. The expression on his face becomes even more determined as he finishes the verse.

> *When you feel the urge within you to submit to earthly fears,*
> *Don't let the faith you're standing in seem to disappear.*

Steve steps forward to join Alvin on the chorus as the musicians build the chord progression to give the message added feeling and strength.

> *Praise the Lord, He can work with those who praise Him,*
> *Praise the Lord, for our God inhabits praise,*
> *Praise the Lord, for the chains that seem to bind you*
> *Serve only to remind you that they*
> *Fall powerless behind you when you praise Him.*

Alvin takes a step backward as the individuals at the keyboards set the stage musically for the second verse. Steve pushes his shoulders back in a pronounced move as he delivers this musical declaration:

> *Satan is a liar, and he tries to make you think*
> *That you're a pauper, when he knows himself*
> *You're a child of the King.*
> *So lift up the mighty shield of faith*
> *For the battle—it's already won.*

Steve continues with the lyrics of the verse. His countenance mirrors the excitement portrayed in his voice as he emphasizes each word.

> *You know that Jesus Christ is risen*
> *And the work's already done.*

As this bold declaration is made, many in the audience stand to their feet and shout words of affirmation like "hallelujah" or "amen"!

Alvin's voice sweeps through the auditorium in a crescendo of sound that begins low and moves up, one note at a time, while he shifts from one foot to the other, eagerly preparing for another chorus of the song. The massive overhead speakers explode simultaneously with the voices of both Steve and Alvin, carrying their voices to every corner of the building.

> *Praise the Lord, He can work with those who praise Him,*
> *Praise the Lord, for our God inhabits praise,*
> *Praise the Lord, for the chains that seem to bind you*
> *Serve only to remind you that they*
> *Fall powerless behind you when you praise Him.*[4]

I have discovered through personal tragedy that my only source of hope is found in Jesus Christ. I have a destiny and a purpose: to help oppressed people everywhere!

"The God of hope has filled me with all joy and peace in believing, and I now abound in hope." Because of that hope, I will face my future with strength, faith, and hope, for I have God beside me!

If you are hurting in some way today or facing some of the challenges or emotions I have discussed in this book, the information I am about to share is for you!

Pain and grief present terrible obstacles in life and often seem insurmountable. I know this from personal experience. As I look back on the past ten years of my life, however, I can point to certain things that have helped to give me strength for today and bright hope for my every tomorrow. It is my prayer that you, too, will find this strength and hope.

## 1. Jesus Christ, our eternal hope.

First of all, I want to reassure you that there is hope for tomorrow. That hope is found in Jesus Christ. When it seemed as if my friends had failed me and I felt so alone, I found what I was searching for in Christ Jesus: love, peace, rest, comfort, and hope.

He loves you and cares about the things that concern you. The Bible says "For God so loved the world, that he gave his only begotten Son, that whosoever believeth in him should not perish, but have everlasting life" (John 3:16 KJV).

In 1 John 1:9 we read "If we confess our sins, He is faithful and just to forgive us our sins and to cleanse us from all unrighteousness."

You can invite Jesus Christ to be your Lord and Savior today by praying this simple prayer: "Lord Jesus, I need You. Please forgive me of all my sins and come into my heart. Be my Lord and Savior from this moment on. Amen."

## 2. You must be fed spiritually.

Just as you need food to nourish your body, you must be fed spiritually. The Bible says, "But grow in grace, and in the knowledge of our Lord and Saviour Jesus Christ" (2 Peter 3:18 KJV). This spiritual growth comes through Bible reading, prayer, and fellowship with other believers.

Read a portion of Scripture from the Bible each day. Spend time talking to God in prayer. Prayer is talking sincerely and honestly with God. Find a local church that teaches the Bible as the Word of God and will teach you how to develop a personal relationship with Jesus Christ.

### 3. You must take care of yourself.

Proper nutrition plays a significant role in your well-being. For a time while I was grieving I didn't eat properly simply because I didn't feel like eating. But when I finally began to take care of myself by nourishing my physical body, I began to look at life differently. Proper nutrition is vital, especially to someone who is suffering grief or the loss of a loved one.

I recently discovered a book that offers some very practical information on proper nutrition titled, *Walking in Divine Health*. Information on how you can secure a copy is included following this section.

### 4. You must get the proper rest.

Getting adequate sleep is just as important as proper nutrition. As you sleep, your body is renewed and refreshed. Take care to get enough rest for your physical and emotional well-being.

### 5. Find some outlet or activity.

Golf became that outlet for me. The physical activity was beneficial and golf became a diversion. Although golf didn't make the pain disappear, it helped to bring balance and relief to my life as I focused on the game instead of my pain.

### 6. Don't neglect your appearance.

Take care of yourself, and don't jeopardize your self-image by neglecting your personal appearance. The routine of getting yourself ready each day will help you stay in touch with life around you.

**7. Don't neglect your professional life.**

Many hurting people withdraw from life as the result of a crisis. Don't impact the loved ones close to you by putting your job in jeopardy.

**8. Give attention to family responsibilities.**

Others close to you may also be hurting. Don't focus so much on your pain that you fail to recognize the suffering of those whom you love. Together, you can help to bring healing to one another's pain and find hope for the future.

**9. Include inspirational reading or listening in your life.**

Take time for inspirational reading or listening. Books and good, wholesome music can have a positive effect upon your mental outlook.

**10. Don't be afraid to get professional help.**

Commit yourself to getting better. Don't be concerned with what others will think. There are many very capable professionals who are specially trained to offer help and support for hurting people. Counselors, ministers, psychologists, psychiatrists, and support groups are available in every city. There are also many charitable organizations like MADD (Mothers Against Drunk Driving), which offer support and assistance. (I have listed some of the organizations and sources that I have come to be aware of.)

## NOTES

**Introduction**
1. "I Bowed on My Knees and Cried Holy," by Lari Goss, © 1989 Word Music (ASCAP). All Rights reserved

**Chapter 1**
1. Sobieski, Regina, *Men and Mourning: A Father's Journey Through Grief*, Mothers Against Drunk Driving, (Rev. 1995), 4.
2. Sadoff, Micky, *America Gets MADD*, Mothers Against Drunk Driving, (1990), 89.

**Chapter 2**
1. F. F. Bosworth, *Christ the Healer* (Grand Rapids, Mich.: Fleming H. Revell, 1982), 195.
2. Ibid., 195–196.
3. Ibid., 196.
4. Ibid.
5. Ibid.
6. "Jesus Lord to Me," words and music by Greg Nelson and Gary McSpadden, © 1981, River Oaks Music Co. / Yellow House Music, International. Copyright secured. All rights reserved.

**Chapter 3**
1. Lehman, D. and Wortman, C., "Long-Term Effects of Losing a Spouse or Child in a Motor Vehicle Crash," Journal of Personality and Social Psychology, (1990).

**Chapter 4**
1. Therese Rando, *Grieving: How to Go on Living when Someone You Love Dies* (San Fransisco, Calif.: Lexington Books, 1988), 36–39.

**Chapter 6**
1. Lewis, C. S., *A Grief Observed*, Seabury Press, (Harper Religious Books), 1989.

## Chapter 7

1. Janice Harris Lord, *Your Grief, You're Not Going Crazy*, Mothers Against Drunk Driving, (Rev. 1995), 10.

## Chapter 10

1. Wolterstorff, N., *Lament for a Son*, Grand Rapids, MI: (Eerdmans Publishing Co., 1987), 96.

## Chapter 11

1. Kenneth W. Osbeck, Amazing Grace (Grand Rapids, Mich: Kregel, 1990), 19.

## Chapter 12

1. "When Answers Aren't Enough," Scott Wesley Brown and Greg Nelson, © 1987 Greg Nelson Music, Pamela Kay Music (admin. by the Copyright Company, Nashville, TN), BMG Songs Inc., Careers-BMG Music Publishing. All rights reserved.

## Chapter 14

1. Billy Graham, Day by Day with Billy Graham, (Minneapolis: World Wide Publications, 1965), April 22.
2. "Praise the Lord" Brown Bannister and Mike Hudson © 1978, Bug and Bear Music, Home Sweet Home Music (admin. by LCS Music Group, Inc.). All rights reserved.

## Chapter 16

1. "Great Is Thy Faithfulness," Thomas O. Chisolm and William M. Runyan, © 1923. Renewal 1951 by W. M. Runyan. Assigned to Hope Publishing Co. All rights reserved.
2. Robert Schuller, The Little Book of Hope, (Nashville: Thomas Nelson Publishers, 1996).
3. Billy Graham, *Day by Day*, April 17.
4. "Praise the Lord," Brown Bannister and Mike Hudson © 1978, Bug and Bear Music, Home Sweet Home Music (admin. by LCS Music Group, Inc.). All rights reserved.

# RESOURCE LIST

MADD
Mothers Against Drunk Driving
511 E. John Carpenter Frwy., Suite 700
Irving, Texas 75062-8187
For victim assistance call: 1-800-GETMADD

H.O.P.E. Builders
Steve Brock Ministries
P. O. Box 13218
Hamilton, Ohio 45013
Office Telephone: 513-856-8124
Fax: 513-856-8616

Trinity Broadcasting Network
T.B.N. 24-Hour Prayer Line: 714-731-1000

Don Colbert, M.D.
Board Certified in Family Practice
Sub-specialty in Preventive Medicine
Extensive training in Tumescent Liposculpting and Hair Transplants
Telephone: 407-331-7007
Author: *Walking in Divine Health*, a helpful, easy-to-read book on health
and nutrition

Dr. Richard D. Dobbins
EMERGE Ministries, Inc.
900 Mull Avenue
Akron, Ohio 44313
Telephone: 330-867-5603
Fax: 330-873-3439
EMERGE is a Christian mental health center dedicated to helping
local churches minister to needs of evangelical believers. Three tiers
of educational opportunities provide training for pastoral counselors.

Audio, video, and printed materials assist churches in equipping constituents for practical Christian living. A psychiatrist, three psychologists, seven counselors, and interns see over 250 people each week. Christian psychiatric care is provided through an inpatient program in a local hospital. EMERGE's board, largely Assemblies of God, represent outstanding men and women from several evangelical groups.

*Steve Brock Show*
Trinity Broadcasting Network
Airs twice each week on T.B.N.
Thursday: 11:30 A.M. (ET)
Friday: 7:30 A.M. (ET)

Helen Pensanti, M.D.
Office Hotline: 714-509-9080

Drs. C. K. & Su Kulasingham
Kulasingham, Inc.
Practice of Psychiatry
Board Certified Psychiatrists
Individual, marital, adolescent, family counseling
Telephone: 513-829-3195

Nutrition Express
P. O. Box 4076
Nutritional supplements mail-order catalog
For a free catalog: 800-338-7979
Fax: 310-784-8522

# ABOUT THE AUTHOR

As a minister of the gospel, Steve Brock presents a message in sermon and song wherever he goes. He has been involved in full-time ministry as both a pastor and evangelist since 1965. Hamilton, Ohio, is currently the home base for Steve Brock Ministries, his evangelistic outreach. He also travels on a regular basis as a featured soloist with the Benny Hinn Miracle Crusades.

Along with his evangelistic ministry, he hosts the *Steve Brock Show* seen around the world on the Trinity Broadcasting Network. He also appears on *This Is Your Day* with Benny Hinn, and serves as guest host from time to time for *Praise the Lord,* also broadcast on Trinity Broadcasting Network.

As a result of his personal tragedy and life experiences, he has established H.O.P.E. Builders, a ministry dedicated to "helping oppressed people everywhere." He and his wife, Pat, along with son Tony, and his wife, Gwen, have joined together to bring a message of hope to the hurting and point them to Jesus Christ, the only hope for today and eternity.